The
MOFFATT
NEW TESTAMENT COMMENTARY

Based on *The New Translation* by the
REV. PROFESSOR JAMES MOFFATT, D.D., LL.D., D.LITT.
and under his Editorship

THE SECOND EPISTLE
OF PAUL TO THE
CORINTHIANS

The Moffatt
New Testament Commentary

MATTHEW
BY THEODORE H. ROBINSON, HON.D.TH., D.D., LITT.D.

MARK
BY B. HARVIE BRANSCOMB, M.A., PH.D.

LUKE
BY WILLIAM MANSON, D.D.

JOHN
BY G. H. C. MACGREGOR, D.D., D.LITT.

THE ACTS OF THE APOSTLES
BY F. J. FOAKES-JACKSON, D.D.

ROMANS
BY C. H. DODD, D.D., F.B.A.

I CORINTHIANS
BY JAMES MOFFATT, D.D., LL.D., D.LITT.

II CORINTHIANS
BY R. H. STRACHAN, D.D.

GALATIANS
BY GEORGE S. DUNCAN, D.D., LL.D.

COLOSSIANS, PHILEMON
AND EPHESIANS
BY E. F. SCOTT, D.D.

PHILIPPIANS
BY J. HUGH MICHAEL, D.D.

THESSALONIANS
BY WILLIAM NEIL, B.D., PH.D.

THE PASTORAL EPISTLES
BY E. F. SCOTT, D.D.

HEBREWS
BY THEODORE H. ROBINSON, HON.D.TH., D.D., LITT.D.

THE GENERAL EPISTLES
BY JAMES MOFFATT, D.D., LL.D., D.LITT.

THE JOHANNINE EPISTLES
BY C. H. DODD, D.D., F.B.A.

REVELATION
BY MARTIN KIDDLE, M.A.
ASSISTED BY M. K. ROSS

THE SECOND EPISTLE OF
PAUL
TO THE CORINTHIANS

BY

R. H. STRACHAN, D.D.

London: HODDER AND STOUGHTON Limited

FIRST PUBLISHED   NOVEMBER 1935
SIXTH IMPRESSION   1954

Made and Printed in Great Britain for
Hodder & Stoughton Limited London, by
The Camelot Press Limited
London and Southampton

EDITOR'S PREFACE

MOFFATT'S NEW TESTAMENT COMMENTARY

THE aim of this commentary is to bring out the religious meaning and message of the New Testament writings. To do this, it is needful to explain what they originally meant for the communities to which they were addressed in the first century, and this involves literary and historical criticism ; otherwise, our reading becomes unintelligent. But the New Testament was the literature of the early Church, written out of faith and for faith, and no study of it is intelligent unless this aim is kept in mind. It is literature written for a religious purpose. ' These are written that ye might believe that Jesus is the Christ, the Son of God.' This is the real object of the New Testament, that Christians might believe it better, in the light of contemporary life with its intellectual and moral problems. So with any commentary upon it. Everything ought to be subordinated to the aim of elucidating the religious content, of showing how the faith was held in such and such a way by the first Christians, and of making clear what that faith was and is.

The idea of the commentary arose from a repeated demand to have my New Testament translation explained ; which accounts for the fact that this translation has been adopted as a convenient basis for the commentary. But the contributors have been left free to take their own way. If they interpret the text differently, they have been at liberty to say so. Only, as a translation is in itself a partial commentary, it has often saved space to print the commentary and start from it.

As everyman has not Greek, the commentary has been written, as far as possible, for the Greekless. But it is based upon a first-hand study of the Greek original, and readers may rest assured that it represents a close reproduction of the original writers' meaning, or at any rate of what we consider that to have been. Our common aim has been to enable everyman to-day to sit where these first Christians sat, to feel the impetus and inspiration of the Christian faith as it dawned upon the minds of the communities in the first century, and thereby to realize more vividly how new and lasting is the message which prompted these New Testament writings to take shape as they did. Sometimes people inside as well as outside the Church make mistakes about the New Testament. They think it means this or that, whereas its words frequently mean something very different from what traditional associations suggest. The saving thing is to let the New Testament speak for itself. This is our desire and plan in the present commentary, to place each writing or group of writings in its original setting, and allow their words to come home thus to the imagination and conscience of everyman to-day.

The general form of the commentary is to provide a running comment on the text, instead of one broken up into separate verses. But within these limits, each contributor has been left free. Thus, to comment on a gospel requires a method which is not precisely the same as that necessitated by commenting on an epistle. Still, the variety of treatment ought not to interfere with the uniformity of aim and form. Our principle has been that nothing mattered, so long as the reader could understand what he was reading in the text of the New Testament.

JAMES MOFFATT.

PREFACE

THE document known as the Second Epistle to the Corinthians
is, in some respects, more difficult and perplexing than any
other of Paul's letters. It presents comparatively few theological problems. The difficulties lie mostly in the interpretation of the movements of thought. The language is sometimes entangled. There are, more than in any other letter,
sudden apparent irrelevancies and unexpected asides. At one
point in the document as we have it (x. 1 ff.) the mood changes
with such disconcerting rapidity that I have been compelled
to side with those who, on internal evidence alone, regard
chapters x. 1–xiii. 10 as belonging to a different letter, written
at a not much earlier date than chapters i.–ix. The same
applies to vi. 14–vii. 1, which is a fragment of a letter earlier
than 1 Corinthians. The impassioned attacks on opponents
contained in these last four chapters, and the vehement utterances of self-defence, are made all the more difficult to understand in the Authorized and Revised English Versions, inasmuch as there are no marks of quotation to denote charges
made against and epithets applied to Paul by his adversaries.
This defect is now supplied in Dr. Moffatt's translation.

In its construction, this letter is in contrast even with
1 Corinthians. In passing from one to the other, as one
commentator remarks, 'we feel as if we had left a park
threaded by footpaths, winding in and out, but all the while
tolerably perspicuous, and had entered upon a trackless
forest.' Accordingly the problem of 2 Corinthians is mostly
the problem of showing why it is that here Paul's mind works
in this particular way. It does so in answer to some sudden
crisis in Corinth, far more serious than was ever foreseen in
the earlier letter. The letter is a very human document, and
I have included in the Introduction a study of the apostle's
personality, particularly as this composite letter reveals it. It
is rich in autobiographical material.

PREFACE

I would acknowledge my indebtedness in particular to the commentaries on the Epistle by the German scholars, H. Windisch and H. Lietzmann ; by A. Plummer (*International Critical Commentary*) ; to the briefer commentary by J. Massie (*Century Bible*). English readers, as well as others, will find the scholarly exposition by J. Denney (*Expositors' Bible*) full of fresh insight into the mind of Paul, and rich in spiritual stimulus.

I am also deeply indebted to Dr. C. A. Anderson Scott, my predecessor in the chair of N.T. Language and Literature at Westminster College, for many criticisms and suggestions, and to the Rev. Hugh Elder, M.A., of Moffat, for valuable assistance in the reading of the proofs.

R. H. STRACHAN.

WESTMINSTER COLLEGE, CAMBRIDGE.
    April 2, 1935.

CONTENTS

INTRODUCTION

COMMENTARY

ix

CONTENTS

INTRODUCTION

INTRODUCTION

I. The Church at Corinth

CORINTH was the leading commercial city in ancient Greece. Situated on the isthmus connecting Northern Greece with the Peloponnesus, and possessed of two harbours, Lechaeum on the west and Cenchreae on the east, it had become the clearing house for sea-borne merchandise passing in either direction, and a considerable number of roads converged upon it. Seamen were thus able to avoid the dangerous voyage round the Peloponnesus, and, also, a more northerly route across the Aegean, in order to escape storms, was rendered possible. Consequently the city acquired an international character. There must have been a considerable inter-mixture of races in its population. Its site would also foster the existence of a variety of religious cults, whose original home, in many cases, was Egypt or Phoenicia. The chief shrine, however, was the Temple of Aphrodite, ideally the Greek goddess of 'the mystery of life and of love that begets life.'[1] But in Corinth the cult appeared in a debased form, due to the accretion of certain non-Greek, Asian, and Phoenician characteristics. The priestess-prostitutes of Aphrodite at Corinth are said to have numbered 1,000. Its luxury and vice gave a word—'corinthianize'—to the Greek language.[2] At one time, the word 'corinthian' was used in English as meaning a rake.[3]

A large proportion of the membership of the Church at Corinth must therefore have been drawn from a motley paganism, with all its heterogeneous standards of life and conduct. Hence arose the variety of questions dealt with in I Corinthians—the meals in pagan temples; the use for food of animals sacrificially slaughtered; the position of

---

[1] J. Harrison, *Prolegomena to the Study of Greek Religion*, p. 314.
[2] Aristophanes, *Frogs*, 133.
[3] Shakespeare, *Henry IV*, Part I, II. iv.

women in the Church ; the case of incest ; the hysteria and disorder at meetings for worship ; the abuses at the Lord's Supper. Also, the tendencies to factiousness and instability have a real psychological basis in both the blend and the clash of racial character to be found in such a cosmopolitan city. An influential section belonged to the considerable Jewish colony, naturally to be found in this commercial centre. The Church was founded as a result of Paul's preaching in the local synagogue (Acts xviii. 1–11).[1]

A serious crisis had arisen at Corinth since 1 Corinthians was written only a few months previously. The second Epistle indicates that a rather sudden revolt had taken place against Paul's apostolic authority, and a determined attempt, nearly successful, was made to undermine his teaching and influence. Serious and important as are the questions dealt with in 1 Corinthians, the whole situation has evidently, after no great lapse of time, developed into one of an entirely different kind. Paul is no longer appealed to by the Corinthian Church to give a ruling on questions of conduct and worship. In chapters x.–xiii., he has vigorously to defend his apostolic authority, and to repel calumnious attacks on his own personal character. These attacks were the result of a visit paid to Corinth by a small body of Jewish Christians who brought credentials from the mother Church at Jerusalem, and claimed an authority superior to that of Paul, whose apostolate they denounced as spurious (xi. 5, 12, 13). It is most important to obtain some clear idea of their mission and attitude. They no doubt fished in already troubled waters, but their arrival was the immediate occasion of the disturbance.

II. THE STRUCTURE OF THE LETTER.—IS IT A LITERARY UNITY ?

The light available for determining the nature of the crisis at Corinth can be obtained only after we have given an answer to the much-disputed question whether the Epistle, as it stands, was originally a literary whole. The discussion has

[1] p. xxvi.

centred mainly around two sections, vi. 14–vii. 1 and x. 1–
xiii. 10, of which the second is by far the more important for
our purpose.

1. vi. 14–vii. 1

There are good internal reasons for the view taken by Dr.
Moffatt, in his footnote, that these verses are a fragment
belonging ' to some other part of Paul's correspondence with
the Corinthian Church.' A sense connexion—at one end with
vi. 13, and at the other with vii. 2—can be found only after
the exercise of the utmost ingenuity. On the other hand, the
connexion between vi. 13 and vii. 2 is quite natural. Denney
(who regards the passage as an integral part of the letter) says
that, in its present position, the passage ' jolts the mind, as
a stone on the road does a carriage wheel.' Many, like the
present writer, feel that the stone was not laid there by Paul's
own hand, and that any connexion of thought with what
precedes and what follows is unrecognizable.

To what other letter do these verses belong ? They would
be quite appropriate as part of the lost letter referred to in
1 Cor. v. 9. The line is sharply drawn between believer and
unbeliever, between good and bad. All incongruous ties are
unreservedly forbidden, and these ties do not refer to sex
relationships alone. The deliverance might easily cause perplexity, and it is remarkable that Paul, referring to a passage in
the lost first letter mentioned in 1 Cor. v. 9, proceeds to correct
just such a mistaken impression as might be derived from the
utterance contained in these verses. He points out that his
words are meant to apply only to ' so-called ' members of the
Church (1 Cor. v. 10–13). The hypothesis, however, has no
manuscript authority, but even the characteristic irrelevancies
and asides of Paul's style can hardly be invoked in support
of the position that this passage is an integral part of the letter.
How such insertions might take place is discussed at the close
of this section. The internal evidence for the hypothesis that
these verses are an insertion will be found in more detail in
the notes.

2. x. 1–xiii. 10[1]

It is quite evident that the state of things in Corinth, reflected in 1 Corinthians, must have become much worse, and indeed critical, before chapters x. 1–xiii. 10 were written. The scathing words recorded in these chapters remind us of passages in Galatians, but the continuous severity of tone is unexampled in Paul's writings. In these chapters he is meeting an emergency, which compels him to exercise to the full his apostolic authority. He mobilizes all his powers of rebuke and denunciation. In ii. 4 Paul speaks of a letter of severe reprimand which he had written. The same letter is evidently referred to in vii. 12. Thus to write had cost him **sore distress and misery of heart,** and **many a tear.** So stern and uncompromising were his words that he says he realized they would hurt, and accordingly had certain misgivings after the letter was out of his hands (vii. 8). We are conscious of a very different atmosphere when we read the opening chapter of 2 Corinthians : ' There has been a storm ; the air is still electric : but the worst is over ' (Massie). Evidently there has been a most serious cleavage, but peace has been secured. His mood is now prevailingly one of glad and grateful reassurance and confident hope. Here and there a certain nervous apprehension appears, and there are some caustic allusions ; but he is able to burst forth into one remarkable paean of praise (ii. 14 ff.), and to say, ' **I am glad to have full confidence in you** ' (vii. 16).

On the other hand, the abrupt and unexpected tone of chapter x. gives the mind much more than a jolt. We feel that all our impressions derived from chapters viii. and ix., with their lyric ending, **Thanks be to God for His unspeakable gift,** are suddenly shattered.

(1) Supporters of the unity of the Epistle urge that there must have been an interval in the writing, during which Paul's whole outlook changed. The suggestions to account for this psychological change are curiously inadequate. It is said to

---

[1] The isolation of these chapters is defended, among many others, by J. H. Kennedy, *The Second and Third Epistles of St. Paul to the Corinthians.*

be the change of mood that comes to an overburdened man whose health is not very robust. He may have had an attack of his recurrent illness (xii. 7). One distinguished commentator suggests a 'sleepless night'! These somewhat desperate suggestions leave out of account the implication that Paul must be ultimately responsible for the final form of this letter. Did he allow nervous exhaustion (undoubtedly present in this letter) or illness to determine the final form of any letter? Chapters i.–ix. are pervaded by peace of mind, and a mood of triumph. Would he have allowed passages written in such different moods to stand together in one letter, which was deliberately intended to serve such an important purpose as to tell his friends of his joy at the reconciliation that had taken place? When he wrote chapters x.–xiii., had he forgotten the misgivings about what would, on this hypothesis, be yet another and previous severe letter? We are asked to believe that the apostle relapsed, even after an interval, but 'for no obvious reason, into the temper of scathing animosity and indignation from which he had just emerged, resuscitating an old quarrel after it had been almost buried.'[1] Paul's temper is passionate, but not choleric and unbalanced.

(2) Others, who hold that the last four chapters are originally part of the letter, explain the abrupt change of tone by asserting that Paul is, in these chapters, addressing a still recalcitrant minority. In chapters i.–ix., he addresses the reconciled majority. If that were so, it is surely very doubtful tactics thus to isolate a minority of rebels, and deliberately to exclude them from all the gracious and generous judgments of the previous chapters. How could Paul have written ii. 10 or ii. 14 with the knowledge that there still existed a rebellious minority? Moreover, he takes no pains whatever to distinguish his two audiences. He takes no steps to warn his readers that the 'you' in the last four chapters has not the same address as the 'you' in chapters i.–ix. In chapters x.–xiii., Paul is not even addressing his Judaizing adversaries alone, nor merely a section which has been affected by their propaganda, but the whole Church. Moreover,

[1] J. Moffatt, *Introduction to the New Testament*, p. 123.

there is no trace of such a powerful minority anywhere else in the letter (see notes on ii. 6). It is quite likely that not every member of the Corinthian Church submitted *ex animo*, or with a good grace, to Paul's censures ; but, of any remaining minority sufficiently active and important to warrant the attacks of chapters x.–xiii., there is not, in the rest of the letter, a single trace. If there had been such a minority, it would hardly have been possible, to speak, as Paul does, of the offender, after his punishment, as so isolated that there is danger lest he be **overwhelmed by excessive remorse** (ii. 7).

(3) There is yet another important consideration which militates against the hypothesis that chapters x.–xiii. are originally part of the letter. In chapters viii.–ix. Paul makes an appeal on behalf of the collection for Palestinian relief. The appeal is made in language which has lifted all Christian appeals of this kind to a new level. Titus is asked to complete the arrangements for this collection, which had been begun before the disturbance, but must have been in abeyance or in confusion during its continuance. The task of Titus would have been rendered almost impossible had he been asked to revive the organization, and to collect voluntary subscriptions, all the time bearing in his hand the philippic of chapters x.–xiii.

(4) Not only has the abrupt change of tone in chapter x. to be accounted for, but some effort has to be made in order, if possible, to identify the severe letter referred to in 2 Cor. ii. 4. Advocates of the unity of the Epistle have sought to identify it with 1 Corinthians. Does 1 Corinthians correspond to the mood of intense agitation in which the severe letter was written ? It is true that the partisan spirit in Corinth, alluded to in 1 Corinthians (i. 10–17 ; iii. 1–17), must have caused Paul much anxiety, but is there anything in his words regarding it that would be likely, on calmer thoughts, to make him doubtful whether he ought to have written them ? Again, he does describe the self-complacency of the Corinthians, in iv. 8–13, with devastating irony, and speaks of ' puffed up ' individuals with a measure of contempt (iv. 18 f.). He

threatens to come with a rod of discipline (iv. 21). The Church is peremptorily enjoined to deal summarily with the incestuous person, and to expel him from their midst (v. 1–8). Paul could not thus have written without anxiety, and even foreboding, but none of these passages seem to be written under the overwhelming nervous strain and deep emotion described as **sore distress and misery of heart, with many a tear.** Moreover, it is not merely of passages in the severe letter that Paul thus speaks. He regretted sending the whole letter (vii. 8). Nor can we believe that Paul's anxiety, even about such a situation as is reflected in 1 Corinthians, would so dominate him as to make it impossible to continue the most promising work of evangelism at Troas, and to compel him to meet the messenger half way, so deeply concerned was he as to the effect produced by the letter (ii. 12 f.). Some have sought to identify the offender, who had also been guilty of some personal wrong done to Paul (ii. 5–11), with the incestuous person of 1 Corinthians. This is entirely out of the question. Paul offers to forgive the offender, as though he had wronged him personally. Surely an offer of personal forgiveness, made to a man guilty of incest, who had wronged a whole Christian community, would be singularly out of place. Moreover, Paul adds that he has written **in order to let you realize before God how seriously you do care for me** (vii. 12). Here again, if he is referring to the case of the incestuous person, any emphasis upon his own standing with the Corinthians is an unwarrantable intrusion, as well as to imply a serious underestimation of the offence and its results.

If we reject the identification of the severe letter with 1 Corinthians, the only alternative is to suggest, either that the letter has been lost, or that we have at least a portion of it preserved in 2 Cor. x. 1–xiii. 10. 2 Cor. i.–ix., and including xiii. 11–13, would therefore be regarded as the letter written after hearing, in Macedonia, from Titus of the good effect produced by the severe letter. It seems to the present writer that from internal evidence alone—for we have no manuscript authority—we are driven to these conclusions.

The hypothesis is further confirmed by various passages in

chapters i.–ix., which give the impression that they refer back to certain utterances in chapters x.–xiii. The following, among others, may be mentioned. The wording of i. 23 suggests that Paul has in mind what he says in xiii. 2—' I will spare no one if I come back.' In ii. 9 and vii. 15 he speaks of his satisfaction with the ' obedience ' for which he asked in x. 6. Even more convincing are the allusions to self-commendation in iii. 1 and v. 12. Chapters x.–xiii. are full of this ' self-commendation,' reluctantly entered upon, but forced on Paul by the attacks on his apostolic standing and teaching. If the last four chapters were written on the same occasion as the rest of the Epistle, Paul has completely violated his assurance of iii. 1–3. It may also be poin.. out that the visit which he had promised and did not pay, thereby incurring the displeasure of the Corinthians (i. 15 ff.), is also mentioned as about to take place in xii. 14 and xiii. 1 (the ' third ' visit). The words of xii. 20 and xiii. 10 give us a fuller statement of the reasons for postponement, which can therefore be stated succinctly in ii. 1—' I decided I would not pay you another painful visit.'[1]

Certain further arguments in detail will emerge in the course of the exposition, but enough has already been said to show that the impossibility of regarding 2 Cor. x. 1–xiii. 10 as part of the same letter as i.–ix. far outweighs the possibility of believing that Paul's whole attitude to the Corinthian Church could thus radically change in the course of a single letter.

Readers may still be inclined to regard the excision of vi. 14–vii. 1, and of the last four chapters, as arbitrary, especially if we make a division at xiii. 10, and attach xiii. 11–13 to chapters i.–ix. How, it may be asked, was it possible thus to dovetail stray portions of one manuscript into the body of another ? If these portions represent torn manuscripts, or surviving pages of manuscripts, of which the rest has been lost, it may be asked, could the tear or the loss always respect the whole of a sentence ? Are we not assuming *four* remarkable coincidences, in each of which the accident

[1] See notes on these passages.

occurred just at the end of one sentence or the beginning of another?

The objection has considerable weight, but only if we assume that the compiler of this particular letter did not feel himself free to restore, where necessary, grammatical connexions. Many of Paul's letters must have been lost, and those that survived were ultimately collected from a few leading Churches to which they were addressed. They would be laid up in their archives, and often probably in disorder. Paul's words would not yet have the value of Holy Scripture, and it is quite conceivable that in giving 2 Corinthians its present form, as part of a general scheme to make a more or less complete collection of his correspondence, the beginnings and endings of fragments would be trimmed to fit what was regarded as their appropriate context. Such work would be done by a copyist. It has been suggested, for example, that the copyist was led, in his rearrangement of fragments, mechanically to connect chapter x. with chapter ix., because ix. 4 mentions an impending visit, and x. 2 also seems to refer to it.

Certain other considerations make it probable that some of Paul's correspondence with the Corinthian Church might be preserved only in parts. We may imagine that some of those who actually passed through the crisis in the Corinthian Church, or their immediate descendants, regarding it as a somewhat discreditable domestic affair,[1] would be disposed to withhold from general circulation both the first letter, referred to in 1 Cor. v. 9, and the third (partly preserved in 2 Cor. x. 1–xiii.). The impressions derived from the first letter had subsequently to be corrected by Paul himself (1 Cor. v. 9 f.). The third letter revealed an even less creditable portion of the Church's history. There is reason to believe that 2 Corinthians in its present form was put into general circulation some considerable time later than 1 Corinthians. It is far from certain that 2 Corinthians was known to any writer earlier than Marcion, who wrote about A.D. 140. Clement of Rome, who writes to the Corinthian Church in A.D. 95, speaks of Paul's ' Epistle ' to Corinth as though he knew of only one. Ignatius writes

[1]Compare Luke's silence on the affair, pp. 63 f.

some ten or twelve years later. Of him it has been said that he must have known the first Epistle almost by heart, so much does its language pervade his own.[1] On the other hand, it is extremely difficult to prove that there are even echoes of 2 Corinthians in his writing. These facts would suggest that the contents of 2 Corinthians were released from the archives of the Corinthian Church at a comparatively late date. It is impossible to tell how much else of Paul's correspondence with Corinth has either been lost, or suffered a fate equivalent to being ' expunged from the minutes.'

III. PAUL'S OPPONENTS IN CORINTH

The facts on which we have to depend for our knowledge of Paul's opponents in Corinth have to be gathered from his own account of them. He writes of them always in a mood of deep resentment and antagonism, and it is permissible to ask, however obnoxious their procedure may have been, whether in every case Paul gave them due credit for their motives. That they were bigoted propagandists, that they had no scruples in invading his spiritual territory, and that their attacks on his personal character were venomous, there can be no doubt. Polemical ardour in religious controversy has often been similarly accompanied, and it would be too much to expect that even Paul could form an entirely just estimate of men who thus defamed him, and had nearly wrecked his work at Corinth.

Are they the same men who created the trouble in Galatia ? The opponents in 2 Corinthians are of Jewish race (xi. 22), and, although the actual question of the Christian attitude towards the requirements of the Law is not debated in detail, the contrast between the Old Covenant and the New in 2 Cor. iii. 6 ff. shows that the general matter at issue is the question of spiritual freedom as against Jewish legalism. There is every probability that the adversaries, as in Galatians, are Judaizers. These are described in Acts xv. 1 : **But certain individuals came down from Jerusalem and taught the brothers**

[1] *The New Testament in the Apostolic Fathers*, p. 67.

that unless you get circumcised after the custom of Moses you cannot be saved. This type of teaching is combated also in Romans. Are we entitled to say that the same influence has been at work in Corinth ?

It has been contended that ' Judaizer ' is not a term appropriate to the opponents in Corinth in the same sense as it may be applied to Paul's antagonists in Galatia.[1] The legalism, it is said, is not of the same type. The issue, however, in Galatians, is not quite so plain as appears at first sight. It is interesting to find that there the opponents' teaching is regarded by Paul as encouraging his converts to relapse into a cult of the forces of nature, from the fear of which the Christian message should have delivered them (Gal. iv. 8 ff.). The opposing teachers demanded the observance of days and months and festal seasons and years, where the reference is to the Jewish feasts. Paul describes these observances as a turning back again to the weakness and poverty of the Elemental Spirits (*stoicheia*).[2] These occasions were determined by the movements of the heavenly bodies, which, in later Judaism, had come to be regarded as themselves the visible embodiments of living and intelligent spiritual beings, a view which Paul seems to have shared with his contemporaries (I Cor. xv. 41).[3] The insistence on the keeping of these feasts, and on the proper astronomical occasion, might easily cause Gentile converts to resume a cult familiar in their pre-Christian days. Teaching of a similar kind reappears in Col. ii. 16–18. It is probable that Paul is referring to this effect of the teaching of the Corinthian Judaizers when he says, I demolish theories and any rampart thrown up to resist the knowledge of God (x. 5). The notion of angelic beings as in control of the forces of nature, or, as Paul would say, ' things in heaven, or in earth, or under the earth,' is not denied ; but this insistence on the ceremonial aspect of the Jewish Law is condemned because it leads to men's thoughts getting seduced

[1] Kirsopp Lake, *The Earlier Epistles of St. Paul*, pp. 226 ff.
[2] See the valuable note in the Moffatt Commentary on *Galatians*, pp. 134–136 ; also pp. 10 f. of the present commentary.
[3] Cf. Philo, *Concerning Giants*, Yonge's translation, I. 331.

from a single devotion to Christ (xi. 3 ; cf. Col. ii. 6–9 ; 1 Cor. viii. 5 f. ; Phil. ii. 10 ff.).

These Corinthian propagandists may be assumed to have put equal emphasis upon the bindingness upon Christians of the moral requirements of the Law. No doubt, they do not represent a purely Palestinian type of Judaism, any more than Paul himself did. The fierce hostility against Stephen was first aroused among diaspora Jews living in Jerusalem (Acts vi. 9), and Saul, himself a diaspora Jew, was commissioned to take steps against the Christians. The diaspora Jews, domiciled among Gentiles, would naturally be more sensitive to any attack on the Law than Jews living in Palestine, where observance of the Law was universal.[1] If, as is most likely, Paul's opponents were converts from diaspora Judaism, they would carry over into the new faith their extreme solicitude for the Law.

It is also probable that these men formerly belonged to a sect of diaspora Judaism which had been influenced by the type of teaching centred in Alexandria. Philo is our chief authority for Alexandrian Judaism, and is himself the exponent of a movement which had made itself felt in religious philosophers of Jewish birth, and must have penetrated beyond academic circles. The movement sought to combine devotion to the sacred tradition of the Law, and, indeed, the whole of the Old Testament, with an outlook on contemporary Hellenistic speculation. The combination was effected in Philo's writing chiefly by a method of sustained allegory.[2] The sacred writings had two meanings, one literal, the other allegorical· Allegorical interpretation, however, while it might free the narrative or utterance from certain moral or intellectual difficulties in the minds of those who practised it, did not impair its historical value or authority.

In one passage, Philo reveals the existence of a school of 'liberal' Judaism, which he himself condemns. He speaks of a class of persons who attach only a symbolic importance

[1] J. Parks, *The Conflict of the Church and the Synagogue*, p. 61.
[2] Paul himself employs the method, in Gal. iv. 22 f., to enforce his own teaching.

to the Scripture. ' The symbolic meaning they seek with every care, but despise the literal meaning. Such laxness I can only deprecate. They ought to be zealous for both—both the exact search for the hidden meaning as well as the punctilious observance of the literal sense."[1] I cite the passage in Dr. Kirsopp Lake's translation, who sees in these symbolists a type analogous to the opposing teachers in Corinth.[2] He assumes two types of opponent, these and Judaizers proper, and thinks that Paul had, in 2 Corinthians and in Galatians, to deal with a Gentile party of ' spiritual perfectionists,' who, as ' spiritual men,' were superior to the authority of the Jewish Law, and even to ordinary principles of morality. They were of the type of liberalism which Philo repudiates.

Is it not more likely that there are not two types, but one, represented not by those whom Philo condemns, but by Philo himself, equally zealous both for the literal sense and the symbolic meaning ? Is it allowable to conjecture that Paul, in chapter iii., by a method learned in a Hellenistic rabbinical school, is antagonizing doctrines founded by his opponents on the story of the shining of the face of Moses by use of a similar method ? Did they see in the radiance a Divine revelation that the glory of the Old Covenant would never fade ?[3]

These men also laid stress on ' visions and revelations '—certain ecstatic experiences which in themselves were regarded as authenticating their mission and message. Otherwise Paul's words in xii. 1 ff. about his own visions are irrelevant to the situation. Philo himself refers to ecstatic experiences of his own which were a means of Divine illumination.[4] Philo's religious experience was indeed of a finer and more worthy texture than theirs. Allegorical interpretation and visions, regarded as Divine illumination, were one thing in Philo's hands and another in theirs, whose main object was, by means of these, to prove points. Philo applied certain safeguards. Philo believed in a ' God who loves to give.' Their perception of hidden meanings, and emphasis on ' visions and revelations,'

[1] *On the Migration of Abraham,* 16.
[2] Kirsopp Lake, *The Earlier Epistles of St. Paul,* pp. 226 ff.
[3] See notes on iii. 14 f.
[4] e.g. *On the Migration of Abraham,* Yonge's translation, II. 50.

was not controlled, we may conjecture, by a real religious sense of responsibility and by the belief that our own highest faculties, including the power of perceiving hidden meanings and responding to ecstatic experiences, are Divine gifts, and must be directed by the Spirit of God. The opponents regarded these as tokens of religious superiority.

This emphasis on ' visions and revelations ' is quite rabbinical. Instances of such visions granted to distinguished patriarchs or rabbis are related in several of the apocryphal writings (e.g. Enoch xxxix. 3). There are numerous ' professional legends ' of distinguished rabbis which tell of a variety of miracles which they worked.[1] That these propagandists had the general approval of the Palestinian Church may be inferred from the influence they obtained over the Corinthian community. In the Jerusalem Church there existed a fanatical Pharisaic section, already mentioned, with whose outlook Paul's opponents might well be in accord. Officially, however, it is disowned (Acts xv. 5, 24). Even although these emissaries brought credentials from the mother Church, the leaders of that Church are not to be held responsible for the attitude they adopted towards Paul and his work, or as approving all the results that followed. In the whole course of the controversy, Paul never once suggests that he is at issue with the Church at Jerusalem.

Paul's opponents would, however, be aided by the presence of an influential section of Jewish Christians in the Church at Corinth. Some of its leading members had belonged to the Jewish synagogue. Crispus, a president of the synagogue, and at least one prominent Jewish proselyte householder, Titus Justus, are mentioned as converts. The names of Priscilla and Aquila are also mentioned, and there must have been others of the rank and file (Acts xviii. 1 ff.). To such people, with their Jewish religious tradition, the moral laxity that had emerged with the entry of ' many of the Corinthians ' (Acts xviii. 8) must have been peculiarly repugnant. The Judaizing emissaries would find, in the minds of some, at least, in that Jewish-Christian section, a soil well suited to, and

---

[1] Cf. G. Foot Moore, *Judaism*, I. 377 f.

perhaps already prepared for, their propaganda. What could be easier or more obvious than to suggest that Paul's doctrine of freedom from the Law was responsible for immorality? Paul accuses his adversaries of 'masquerading' as ministers of righteousness (xi. 15). This was probably their own title for themselves, and is a significant description of men who regarded the Law as the one and only sanction for morality. Moreover the Gentile section would be inclined to resent Paul's interference (as in 1 Cor. vi. 1–11, viii. 1–13 ; 2 Cor. vi. 14–vii. 1) with pagan customs which lay at the foundation of social life. Those who had been guilty of gross immorality might also be ill-disposed towards Paul and vindictive. His opponents fished in already troubled waters. But neither the emissaries, nor the Jewish Christians who sided with them, could actually have foreseen the ultimate result of undermining Paul's authority, and that they would fail to impose their own instead. The situation evidently got completely out of control, and, degenerating into a condition of moral anarchy, had become a serious menace to the continued existence of a Christian Church at Corinth.[1]

In thus discrediting Paul, these Judaizers had only succeeded in deposing Christ from His true place in Christian thought and worship. Paul, therefore, fiercely attacks them as 'interlopers,' as preaching 'another Jesus,' a different 'spirit,' and another 'gospel' (xi. 4). He estimates their message, not merely by its content, but by its actual baneful results. They no doubt quoted traditional sayings of Jesus like those preserved in Matt. v. 17–19, or Matt. xxiii. 2 f., against his doctrine of freedom from the Law.[2] Paul sweeps even such a powerful Christian legalism aside. The Christ he

[1] Cf. pp. 69 f.
[2] It has been suggested that the sayings preserved in Matthew's Gospel asserting the validity of the Jewish Law (Matt. v. 17–19, xxiii. 2 f.), and emphasizing Jesus' mission to 'the lost sheep of the house of Israel ' (Matt. xv. 24), which stand side by side with a clear recognition of the Gentile mission (xxviii. 19 f.), were derived from a cycle of tradition representing a Judaistic reaction against the liberalism of Paul in the matter of the Gentile mission and the observance of the Law (Streeter, *The Four Gospels*, pp. 511 f.). The Palestinian Christians, at the first, zealously observed the Law of Moses and worshipped in the Temple (Acts ii. 46, iii. 1, v. 42).

preaches is not a ' Christ after the flesh,' whose authority over men is external (v. 16).[1] The Judaistic Christ is not the ' image of God.'

We may thus gain a general impression of the issue between Paul and his opponents. The personal attacks made on his character are simply the result of that degeneration of atmosphere which the *odium theologicum* so often produces. As a preacher, they said, he was miserably ineffective (x. 10) ; bold only at a distance (x. 1) ; did not know his own mind, and said ' yes ' and ' no ' in the same breath (i. 17, 18) ; his attitude to his converts was tyrannical (x. 8) ; his flight from Damascus was cowardly and ludicrous (xi. 32 f.) ; he accepted no maintenance because he was not sure of his own apostleship (xi. 7, 9) ; yet he made something out of it, getting his share in an underhand way, through his agents (vii. 2, xii. 17 f.) ; the man is constantly ' commending himself ' and claiming a heaven-born authority (iii. 1) ; he must be crazy (v. 13). At the same time, we cannot claim that Paul himself is blameless and without prejudice in his estimate of his opponents. They adulterate the gospel, he says, like fraudulent wine-merchants (ii. 17, iv. 2, xi. 3, 13). Their message is a diabolical caricature of the truth (xi. 14). They demand maintenance in overbearing and insolent ways (xi. 20). Their ministerial commission is from Satan (xi. 15). If the invaders' account of Paul's character and teaching is the outrageous distortion of bigotry, we must also be prepared to allow that Paul's own account, in the heat of controversy, of the character and motives of his opponents is here and there coloured by his completely justifiable resentment against the grave injury they had been the means of doing to himself and to the Church he had founded at Corinth.

[1] The situation created was much the same as when to-day Jesus' words about non-resistance are quoted as an argument against the use of force in all circumstances, or His words ' Swear not at all ' against any taking of oaths.

IV. A Human Document

None of Paul's letters is so rich in material enabling us to form a conception of the apostle's personality. It has been said that Paul is everywhere ' vehemently present ' in his writing. This is outstandingly true of the present Epistle. The causes of its entangled style and the swift changes of mood lie in the peculiarly difficult circumstances which Paul encountered in Corinth, and in the characteristic and varied response which he made to these, not only in action, but in feeling. This letter has been well described as ' a tumult of contending emotions.' At one time Paul's affection for, and pride in, his new-made converts is wounded to the quick ; at another he is filled with joy that they have again given him their confidence and obedience. Sometimes we feel that his self-respect has been injured ; sometimes we are made to realize how repugnant to him is all self-assertion. The letter is an artless and unconsciously autobiographical description of the ways in which Paul was accustomed to meet slander and calumny, physical danger and bodily suffering, disloyalty and ingratitude, from those for whom he had given of his best, the disillusionment and disappointment that invaded his spirit from time to time. We are at liberty to assess the moral quality of these reactions in the same light in which Paul himself always sought to live. He is at all times sincere ; never more so than when he says **we have all to appear without disguise** before the tribunal of Christ (v. 10). There are no disguises in this letter. The fierce accusations ; the abrupt transition of thought and feeling ; phrases like, ' belongs to Christ ' (x 7), ministers of righteousness (xi. 15), seized on the very lips of his opponents and flung back at them ; the pain caused by his Corinthian friends quickly exchanged for a mood of glad confidence and thanksgiving—all these are faithful reflections of his feelings at any particular moment. Moods of anger and love, anxiety and hope, joy and sorrow, follow one another, like waves on a troubled sea ; sometimes tossing themselves one upon the other. He describes with great vividness and frankness one moment of real emotional conflict, and tells how he was compelled to cut short a promising bit of work at Troas, because ' I got no relief from the strain of things, even when I reached Macedonia ; it was trouble at every turn, wrangling all round me, fears in my own mind ' (vii. 5). Is it remarkable that plans were changed with apparent ' fickleness ' (i. 17) ? At least, so it appeared to the impercipient Corinthians. Nor must we leave out of account the fact that the profound mental disturbance caused by the happenings at Corinth must have had its effect upon Paul's general health at this time. A good deal of the fierceness and bitterness of tone in the four later chapters must be put down to sheer nervous exhaustion. Yet, in spite of these conflicting moods, Paul still remains master of himself. The moods vary intensely and constantly. ' Yet there is neither vacillation nor contradiction. As each is roused and warranted by circumstances, so he remains master of all. He throws his whole being into every emotion, and he is always the same.'[1]

Paul is so little the slave of conflicting moods that this Epistle displays some of his finest qualities as an administrator. It is a remarkable fact that the Corinthian community, in Paul's absence and in spite of his hurried and apparently ignominious leaving on the occasion of the ' painful visit,'[2] should by itself have been able to bring order out of chaos in response to his stern appeal and withering criticism.[3] In spite of the gravity of the situation and the breakdown of local organization, Paul still wields his apostolic authority so as ultimately to leave even these serious matters to the decision and judgment of the community itself. Thereby alone, as he recognizes, a really stable solution could be obtained. He does not forget, even amid such happenings, that capacity for moral judgment, only to be developed in moral freedom, is the greatest gift that can come to this disordered community. The only way to preserve moral freedom is to make those who exercise it responsible for its preservation. ' Why judge ye not of yourselves what is right ? ' (Luke xii. 57; cf. x. 36). He will not lord it (i. 24) over men's faith. The picture which

---

[1] C. Weizsäcker, *The Apostolic Age*, English translation, I., p. 374.
[2] pp. 62 ff.   [3] ii. 6 ff.

this letter affords of a man who, on the one hand, is able, at a distance and by means of a letter, to restore order in Corinth, and, on the other, can be visited by qualms of conscience and serious misgiving about its tone, reveals a powerful personality whose greatness is rooted in humility. The ultimate stability of his work in Corinth is a concrete illustration of the great principle he lays down in the earlier Epistle :—' Other foundation can no man lay than that is laid ' (I Cor. iii. 9–15). The ordeal by fire which tries every man's work, has come even more quickly than Paul expected, and the structure he reared has survived.

The real secret of this mastery of moods and events is revealed in the fact that the responsible sense of his apostleship, and of an apostolic message entrusted to him, is never absent. At several points where he is perforce occupied with matters that must have been so vexatious or repugnant, or merely trifling, as to drive a lesser man in upon himself and keep him entangled in fruitless and trivial controversy, Paul suddenly shakes himself free. The gospel entrusted to him and his pastoral responsibility towards the Corinthians assume control of his mind. A notable example is the way in which, in the midst of a controversial passage, he unexpectedly utters words which reveal the heart of his whole evangel and the character of his ministry, particularly in one pregnant sentence—**He entrusted me with the message of His reconciliation** (v. 14–21). In the course of dealing with the mundane but anxious matter of finance, his eyes suddenly fix themselves upon the lavishness and self-forgetfulness of the Incarnation (viii. 9). ' The look that has just been fixed on the near-lying scene passes immediately to the distant prospect ; from the surface it everywhere penetrates into the depths.'[1] Along with Paul's firm hold on the realities of the outward situation there goes a genuine ' mysticism.' Even in his most anxious and despairing moments, how very much more real than the outward situation, ' things seen,' are ' things unseen and eternal ' (iv. 18). **The slight trouble of the passing hour** are the words of a truly practical mystic who is never separated

[1] C. Weizsäcker, *op. cit.*, I., p. 375.

from his religion. His attitude towards the varied happenings and demands of this present life is more sympathetic and penetrating, but much less tenacious and absorbing, than the attitude of those **whose eyes . . . are on the seen.**

It seems strange that it should ever have been possible to accuse of double-dealing[1] a man of such transparent frankness. His opponents make the accusation that he is **humble enough to your face when he is with you, but outspoken enough when he gets away from you** (x. 1; cf. x. 10). The insinuation is born of malice, but is ultimately based upon a misinterpretation of his actual character. Paul had indeed two sides to his character. The Epistle to Philemon, written to a personal friend, reveals a genius for making and keeping friends, not without a parallel in others of his letters. It also displays his gift of humour and his playfulness, and a persuasive power of Christian appeal alike to a slave and his master. It is written as though he spoke with Philemon face to face. There Paul is sure of his ground, whereas in the final chapters of 2 Corinthians it is trembling beneath his feet. Yet the same power of persuasive appeal returns in chapters viii. and ix., when the breach has been restored. When he talks with men face to face, especially his spiritual children, and he is sure of his ground, all the native courtesy and winningness of his personality are uppermost. These are not moments for a display of spiritual authority. Any man might read, but no man could write, 1 Cor. xiii. without being himself ' changed into the same image.'

Paul himself is aware that his tone and attitude towards those who are under his pastoral care when he is writing to them would alter if he were face to face with them. **Would that I could be with you at this moment, and alter my tone, for I am at my wits' end about you !** (Gal. iv. 20). Here again he is writing at a distance, but is grievously disturbed that his apostolic authority, very real and dear to him as Christ's own gracious commission and trust, has been brought into disrepute and flouted. The torrent of passionate

---

[1] In what follows I have made use of some sentences from my book *The Individuality of St. Paul*, pp. 282 ff.

conviction that he has been commissioned by Christ Himself breaks in fierce invective upon the obstacle so wilfully and contemptuously placed in its channel. At times the old fanaticism of the Jewish persecutor remains as ' a different law in his members ' (Rom. vii. 23). He speaks of his opponents as these dogs, **the incision-party,** who mutilate themselves (Phil. iii. 2). On one occasion, he suggests that the mutilation of circumcision, on which they pride themselves, might as well be deeper, so that they become like the priests of Cybele (Gal. v. 12 [Moffatt]).[1] Luke, on the other hand, records that, when ordered to be struck on the mouth by the high priest Ananias, Paul retorted, ' God shall smite thee, thou whited wall ! ' Then, in a moment, we find him expressing sincere regret for his words, and explaining that he had not recognized who had given the order.[2] Paul was capable of these swift transitions of mood. He knew, equally well with his opponents, that it is one thing to write a strong letter in defence of a great cause, another to be face to face with those who were being led astray, and for whose sake he was willing to suffer much. Then his instinct was to beseech and plead. He had a yearning even for stupid and easily led people—**what is foolish in the world.** Had not God chosen them **to shame the wise ?** (I Cor. i. 27). When they made these charges of double-dealing, were his opponents not stung by the success of Paul's own powers of immediate personal appeal against their own failure to capture the same hearts ? Thus even the envious spirit which lurks behind such charges has uttered both truth and falsehood. Slander, like caricature, if it is to be effective must have some relevance to its subject. Even the slander, ' a gluttonous man and a wine-bibber,' has at least slain any conception of Jesus as a pale Galilean ascetic. The occasions, as it has been said, which

[1] Dr. Moffatt's translation here is, I think, too strong. Paul's words are coarse, but he does not express a wish. Rather, he suggests that emphasis on circumcision as a physical mutilation with which God is well pleased, implies a religious mentality no different from that of pagan religions which enjoin the practice of castration. ' They might as well go the whole length.'

[2] Acts xxiii. 3 f. See Kirsopp Lake, Moffatt Commentary on *Acts, in loco.*

provoke the taunts of our enemies, are often those which may cause perplexity to our friends.

In bringing their charge of duplicity, Paul's enemies may not have overlooked certain characteristics of Paul's style which are most vividly described by Jerome. Jerome is referring more particularly to the Epistles to the Romans and the Galatians, where Paul, as he says, is *totus in certamine.* His words, however, are also peculiarly applicable to the style of 2 Cor. x.–xiii. 'Whenever I read him,' he says, ' I seem to hear not words but peals of thunder. When he cites proofs from the Old Testament, we observe how dexterous and sagacious he can be, with a faculty for disguising what he is doing. His words seem simple, the utterances apparently of a guileless and unsophisticated person, incapable either of employing or repelling stratagems. Yet, wherever one looks, lightnings flash. He sticks to his point, keeps hold of what-ever he touches, turns his back in order to conquer, simulates flight in order to slay.'[1] Jerome goes on to refer to the charge that the Old Testament citations so often mean one thing, but in Paul's hands they mean another. Has Jerome here put his finger on another of the specious reasons why Paul might be accused of duplicity ? It is, however, hardly an adequate defence against such a charge to say, as Jerome does, *aliud est docere discipulum, aliud adversarium vincere !*[2]

Occasionally we hear the Jewish aristocrat speak, who is proud to trace his descent from the royal tribe of Benjamin (xi. 22). Paul boasts that he is a pure-blooded Hebrew (Phil. iii. 5). Sometimes he displays what has been called ' a militant sense of personal dignity.'[3] This mingles with, and is most often absorbed in, the larger and nobler conscious-ness of Christian apostleship. Just as he once regarded him-self as representing and defending the finest spiritual traditions of the Jewish race as a ' prince with God,' so now, as an apostle of Christ, he is filled with a wondering yet humbler consciousness that he has been chosen as an ambassador on behalf of Christ, in whom all ' the promises of God ' are

---

[1] *Ep.* xlviii. (Migne, I. 223).   [2] Cf. notes on iii. 13.
[3] W. M. Macgregor, *Christian Freedom*, p. 51.

fulfilled. He is daring enough to think of himself as a second Moses, with a superior glory in his heart, in the presence of which the glory on Moses' face after communing with God on Sinai is but a fading ray. He is bold enough, by a dexterous use of rabbinic allegorizing, to assert that Moses himself veiled his face because he knew that the dazzling glory it bore must wane (iii. 13). Paul, the aristocrat, must have with difficulty repressed the ' natural man ' within him, when his Judaizing opponents spoke of Peter, James, and John, men of another social rank than he, as the **pillars** (Gal. ii. 9) on which the Church of Christ rested, and on which he himself must lean; more particularly when he remembered their noble attitude towards himself. His supreme boast is that he claims his spiritual office alongside them. He, too, is an apostle of Christ ' by the will of God ' (i. 1 ; cf. Gal. i. 1 f.).

Dr. Moffatt's justifiable rendering of ' we,' ' us,' and ' our ' in the traditional English version of Paul's letters by ' I,' ' me,' and ' my ' where the Greek is plural, may seem to suggest a considerable strain of egotism. In Hellenistic Greek, ' we ' is often used where ' I ' is intended, and, similarly, ' our,' meaning ' mine.'[1] Paul, however, speaks of himself so frequently in the first person in this letter because there is what may be called a Divine necessity that he should do so. His own character and his apostolic authority are the leading subjects of discussion, and they are forced upon him. He is not engaged in mere self-vindication, although he is apparently accused of a habit of ' self-commendation.' Paul's character and apostolic authority were crucial matters, and very vital to the situation at Corinth. There Paul, and he alone, was Christ's **spokesman** (xiii. 3) in word and example. Other missionaries throughout the centuries since, responsible for a Christian community like an ' island in a sea of paganism,' become similarly conscious of their supreme importance as ' ensamples to the flock.'

---

[1] In papyri documents there is apparently an arbitrary interchange of singular and plural. In the New Testament the usage is a problem for the exegete, not for the grammarian. In general, it may be said that when Paul does use the first person singular (e.g. x. 1) he is expressly calling attention to his own personal consciousness (J. H. Moulton, *Grammar of New Testament Greek*, I. 87).

These personal matters also had a universal significance, reaching far beyond Corinth. Paul did lay unique stress on his apostolic authority.[1] To reject it meant the acceptance of a Christ who was no more than the finest flower of Judaism ; a Divine Being and a Saviour He might be, but only of those who were ready to assent to the ritual and institutional system of Judaism. Paul was the means of saving Christianity from becoming a Jewish sect, instead of, as it is, the universal fulfilment of Jewish religion. We worship, not Jesus of Nazareth, but the risen and exalted Christ.

Paul's defence of his apostolic authority has much more than a local significance. This self-assertion is forced upon him. He writes **not to prove I am a success, that is not the point, but that you should come right, even if I seemed to be a failure (xiii. 7).** All great missionaries have been content that their converts should cease to listen to them if only they will listen to Christ. Self-disclosure and all forms of mere ' exhibitionism ' are distasteful to Paul. It is always painful to lay bare his inmost soul, a pain which he sometimes tries to conceal by irony (xii. 12 ff.) ; yet, say what he will, his individuality is never divorced from his words. Sometimes he is conscious of a desire that it should be so. **You don't have to read between the lines of my letters ; you can understand them. Yes, I trust you will understand the full meaning of my letters as you have partly understood the meaning of my life (i. 13 f.).**

That Paul's personality is so vigorously apparent in his writing, is of much more than religious significance. His letters are not literary productions, yet all unconsciously Paul set his stamp on the subsequent history of Greek literature. ' The next great romantic after Plato is St. Paul,'[2] if romanticism is the appropriate term for those waves of fresh emotion, always accompanied by a new living interest in ' things unseen '—whether these lie in the region of art, poetry, or religion—which are poured upon human life. Wordsworth describes one form of romanticism when he speaks of

[1] Cf. pp. 41 ff.
[2] H. J. C. Grierson, *The Background of English Literature*, p. 273.

a sense sublime
Of something far more deeply interfused
Whose dwelling is the light of setting suns,
And the round ocean, and the living air,
And the blue sky, and in the mind of man.

The romanticism of Paul is less mystical and far more personal, its content far less vague. It is the inevitable expression of the firm conviction based upon a Divinely revealed truth that the Great New Age, the 'world to come' foretold by prophets, has arrived in the historical person of Jesus Christ, now risen, ascended, and reigning in the universe. ' All things have been created through Him, and unto Him, and He is before all things, and in Him all things consist.' ' Our light affliction which is for a moment worketh for us more and more exceedingly an eternal weight of glory ; while we look not at the things which are seen, but at the things which are not seen ; for the things that are seen are temporal ; but the things that are not seen are eternal.' Paul has no eye for blue skies or sunsets ; yet the marvel is that this new romanticism reacted inevitably on the form in which it was compelled to express itself—namely, the Greek language. Wilamovitz Moellendorf, in a remarkable passage,[1] points out that Paul's influence on the language was both disintegrating and vitalizing. Paul's letters, like all letters, are written in absence, but they are like weapons in the hand of a man who is actively present. The style was indeed the man. Paul's use of the Greek language is not a means of its deterioration. The spirit that was in him gave it new life. Moellendorf, a very distinguished classical scholar, gives as his considered opinion that Paul is a ' classic of Hellenism.' His Christian faith, compelled to utter itself in the Greek language, created a new style at a period when style had become manner. Paul's Greek models itself on no school, and has no prototype in earlier literature. Yet his Greek remains Greek, and his vocabulary and style are comparatively little Hebraized—a contrast with the Gospels. The reason is, says Moellendorf, that Paul's thinking, the living instrument of the new

[1] *Die Griechische und Lateinische Literatur und Sprache* (*Die Kultur der Gegenwart*, I. vii.), pp. 157 ff. I owe the reference to Professor Grierson.

romantic spirit of Christianity, comes direct from the heart ' spontaneously in a precipitate gushing stream. . . . At last, at last, once more does someone speak in Greek out of a fresh, inward experience of life. That experience is his faith. He is sure of the hope within him, and his glowing love embraces all mankind, to whom in order to bring healing, he will gladly throw away his life. A fresh life of the soul springs up in all places whither his feet carry him. It is as a substitute for his personal activity that he writes his letters. This epistolary style is Paul himself, and no other. . . . To him all literature is a bauble ; he is without any artistic vein. All the greater is the estimate we must form of the artistic effects which he yet achieves.' The conventional forms, the polished beauty, and the commonplaces of the Hellenic world are gone, and instead we experience the quickening power of a certain literary uncouthness, which is apparent even in the English rendering, and yet is adequate to the thought and feeling expressed.

We become conscious of a certain irony of history, when we are thus reminded of a very remarkable literary by-product of Paul's passionate Christian message. In his writing there is not a blade of green grass, not a single pastoral scene, not so much as a glimpse of the sea, though he had been in many storms. Therein lies a great contrast with the speech of Jesus. Yet Paul, with all his formlessness, writes often with sublimity. He revived the Greek tongue. By means of it he proclaims that God can come to men, and men to God, by a clearer and simpler way than the Hellenic ' wisdom of this world ' can afford her art and poetry and philosophy. **Has not God stultified the wisdom of the world?** (I Cor. i. 21). It is a very hard judgment—some might say the utterance of a Philistine. But it was uttered under the shadow of a tremendous conviction that, since God had come in Jesus Christ, His coming again finally to gather up the fruits of His Son's sacrifice and suffering would not be long delayed. To turn from idols is ' to serve a living and true God, and to wait for His Son from heaven.' Foolishness, no doubt, this despising of culture. But history has shown it to be the foolishness of God which is wiser than men.

INTRODUCTION

V. Outline of the Story of Paul's Relations with the Corinthian Church

The following arrangement of events is partly conjectural, but is accepted as the chronological basis of the present commentary. Opinions differ within a year or two as to the date when the Church was founded, and when the first Epistle was written. These are properly matters of discussion in connexion with the first Epistle. The date of 2 Corinthians is determined by the date assigned to 1 Corinthians. The strong probability is that an interval of less than a year separated both parts of the second letter from the first. Portions enclosed in square brackets indicate matters which are only more or less probable.

1. Paul leaves Athens, visits Corinth, and founds the Church. The visit lasted 1½ years. [Date : spring of A.D. 55] (Acts xviii. 1 ff.).

2. Paul leaves Corinth and settles in Ephesus (Acts xviii. 18 f.).

3. Paul sends a letter, now lost [2 Cor. vi. 14–vii. 1 may be a fragment of it. Titus is its bearer] (1 Cor. v. 9).

4. 'Members of Chloe's household' (1 Cor. i. 11) bring to Paul at Ephesus unsatisfactory news about the existence of factions at Corinth.

5. A letter from Corinth reaches Paul, asking his ruling and guidance on certain points affecting the ordering of worship and relationships with Gentile society (1 Cor. vii. 1).

6. In reply, Paul writes 1 Corinthians, at or near Easter (1 Cor. xvi. 8) [A.D. 57]. Titus and another are the bearers (2 Cor. xii. 18) [Titus returns to Ephesus].

7. Timothy is sent to Corinth, after despatch of 1 Corinthians [and before return of Titus], on a special mission (1 Cor. iv. 17).

8. Meantime a very serious crisis arises in Corinth, fomented by the arrival of Judaizing emissaries. Paul's authority is defied (2 Cor. x. 10, xi. 23, xii. 16 f.). Timothy, on arrival, finds this situation [and is quite unable to deal with it]. He returns with bad news to Ephesus.

9. On receiving Timothy's report, Paul pays a brief visit

to Corinth, in order to deal with the emergency in person. This is the ' painful visit ' (2 Cor. ii. 1). He is compelled, after a distressing experience, to return to Ephesus.

10. Paul writes, and sends by Titus to Corinth, a letter of severe castigation and remonstrance (2 Cor. ii. 4). A considerable portion of this letter is preserved in 2 Cor. x.–xiii. 10. Titus is instructed to meet Paul at Troas.

11. According to the plan outlined in 1 Cor. xvi. 5 ff., but after some delay caused by the sudden visit to Corinth, he leaves Ephesus for Macedonia, probably visiting the Churches of the Lycus valley on his way. He reaches Troas, and fails to find Titus. He leaves Troas for Neapolis (the port of Philippi) in order to meet Titus on his way (2 Cor. ii. 12 f.).

12. Paul meets Titus, and receives a most encouraging report. The crisis is at an end (2 Cor. vii. 6–16).

13. Paul writes 2 Cor. i.–ix. and sends it from Macedonia by Titus, accompanied by two others.

14. Paul himself reaches Corinth. The time of his stay there—three months, according to Acts—and the fact that he was planning to leave for Syria, i.e. at a time when the long voyage was possible (Acts xx. 3), would indicate that he came to Corinth later than early November [A.D. 57].

The actual dates are conjectural within a narrow limit, but to determine the year is not nearly so important as to realize that first and second Corinthians were written in the same year, and that all the events (4–14 as above) took place between some date shortly before Easter and the very late autumn of that year; say, within seven or eight months. Paul's ' painful visit '[1] to Corinth from Ephesus and his return might, in favourable weather, occupy less than three weeks.

[1] pp. 62 ff.

COMMENTARY

In the pages that follow, the text of the Epistle is arranged in accordance with the conclusions reached regarding its structure (pp. xiv.–xxi.). The Epistle in its present form seems to contain portions of *three* letters to the Corinthians :—

I. A Fragment of an Earlier Letter; written before 1 Corinthians. (vi. 14–vii. 1.)

II. The Severe Letter ; written to meet a serious revolt against Paul's teaching and authority. (x.–xiii. 10.)

III. A Letter from Macedonia ; written after the crisis had passed, and peace was restored. (i.–ix.)

COMMENTARY

I. A FRAGMENT OF AN EARLIER LETTER
(vi. 14–vii. 1)

vi. 14–vii. 1 : THE CHURCH HAS WALLS

vi.

[Keep out of all incongruous ties with unbelievers.   14
    What have righteousness and iniquity in common,
       or how can light associate with darkness ?
    What harmony can there be between Christ and Belial,   15
       or what business has a believer with an unbeliever ?
    What compact can there be between God's temple and 16
       idols ?

For we are the temple of the living God—as God has said,

> *I will dwell and move among them,*
> *I will be their God and they shall be My people.*

Therefore *come away from them,*   17
   separate, saith the Lord,
   touch not what is unclean ;
   then I will receive you,
I will be a Father to you,   18
   and you shall be *My sons and daughters,*
   saith the Lord almighty.

vii.

As these great promises are ours, beloved, let us cleanse our- 1
    selves from everything that contaminates either flesh or
    spirit ; let us be fully consecrated by reverence for God.]

This bracketed paragraph is to be regarded as belonging to
some other letter.[1] That it is an insertion is suggested, apart
from its content, by the way in which vi. 13 and vii. 2 follow
naturally on one another. The broken edges fit so closely

---

[1] For the arguments in favour of the hypothesis that it belongs to
the earlier letter mentioned in 1 Cor. v. 9, see p. xv.

3

that there is little room for doubt. The fragment may well
14 belong to the letter, now lost, referred to in 1 Cor. v. 9.[1] As
the translation shows, the demand is even more uncompromising, and has a wider sweep than the ' Be not unequally yoked
together ' of the A.V. **Keep out of all incongruous ties with
unbelievers.** Other references in 1 Cor. vi. 8, 10, 14 ff. shed
light on the nature of these ties. The history of Christian
missions repeats itself. Paul is here dealing with the same
kind of influences and relationships, carried over from the old
pagan life, that still affect the newly made Indian or Chinese
convert. In his bare pronouncement here, Paul takes no
account of the real conflict of loyalties that might arise in
Corinth, and still arises in the mission field ; as, for example,
when a wife becomes Christian and her husband remains a
pagan ; or the case of the low-caste Christian who formerly
made his living by service in a heathen temple ; or the participation in pagan ceremonies on social occasions. These
15 cannot be resolved by such an utterance as, **What business
has a believer with an unbeliever ?** ; or by citations from
16- the prophetic writings. Paul's former Pharisaic training has
18 had its influence in the use he makes of the words, **touch not
what is unclean ; then I will receive you.** It is not surpris-
ing that he is compelled to deal with the subject more fully
in 1 Corinthians, and has to correct wrong impressions (1 Cor.
v. 9 ff.) that might be obtained from such language as he uses
in this fragment. **Belial** (verse 15) is a name used frequently,
in the inter-testamental Jewish literature, for the Devil.

Even after the subsequent amplifications of his earlier
language, when he recognizes how complicated the problem
was for many of his converts, Paul still leaves us with the
necessity, in the mind and conduct of the Christian man, for
these sharp separations between **righteousness** and **iniquity,
believers** and **unbelievers,** which are the basis of Christian
Puritanism.[2] Bunyan, in his quaint way, allegorizes the
' snuffers ' of Solomon's Temple. ' If our snuffs,'[3] he says,

---

[1] p. xv.
[2] See Denney, *The Second Epistle to the Corinthians*, pp. 237 ff.
[3] i.e. the part of the wick charred by the flame.

'are our superfluities of naughtiness, our snuffers then are those righteous reproofs, rebukes, and admonitions, which Christ has ordained to be in His house for good.' But he adds, ' They must be used wisely. It is not for every fool to handle snuffers at or about the candles, lest perhaps, instead of mending the light, they put the candle out.'[1] Bunyan's reservation is wise, but, like Paul, he recognizes that the Church has walls, and that the boundary-line between right and wrong must be drawn, where it is possible and desirable to do so.

This Christian Puritanism is no abstract theory of life, founded on a narrow theology, but is born of a realistic sense of the value of individual human lives. Mark Rutherford says, ' Religion is dead when the imagination deserts it. When it is alive, abstractions become visible and walk about the roads.'[2] These abstractions, righteousness and iniquity, in the present passage are ' visible ' to Paul. Paul is thinking in terms of persons whom he knows, and for whose welfare he cares. They are ' alive and walk about the roads.' In his treatment of these moral questions at Corinth he thinks in terms of a man guilty of incest (1 Cor. v. 1) ; of wives, husbands, and children (1 Cor. v. 10 ff.) ; of slaves (1 Cor. v. 21 ff.) ; of Christian litigants in a pagan court (1 Cor. vi. 1 ff.) ; of persons of ' enlightened mind ' forgetful of their ' weaker brethren ' (1 Cor. viii. 10).

> Only like souls I see the folk thereunder,
> Bound who should conquer, slaves who should be kings.

In his demand for a clear-cut separation between ' believers ' and ' unbelievers,' Paul is not thinking in terms of an abstract theology, but of actual personal relationships in the life of a pagan city. He knows that there must be some visible obedience to the command, *Come away from them, separate, saith the Lord*, if the evangelizing task is to be accomplished. The boundary-line between Church and world tends to become dangerously obscured. The gospel of God's immanence, whose burden is that God is already within even the worst of men,

---

[1] *Solomon's Temple Spiritualized*, Offor's ed., III. 488.
[2] *John Bunyan*, p. 231.

5

is a half-truth and has in itself no redemptive power. The Divine spark is not the same as the Divine fire. Christian men who tolerate **incongruous ties with unbelievers** cannot bring other men where they themselves are. The moral separation between Christ and the natural man must be plain, while at the same time the lives as well as the words of Christian men must have an ' inviting language,' which is the burden of the twelfth chapter of Romans. Yet Paul is deeply conscious of the moral demands of the Christian gospel, and of the obligation that rests on every Christian man to refrain from exercising any un-Christlike tolerance towards those whose way of living and moral outlook are a serious danger to their fellows, as well as to themselves. ' Knaves and cowards and cunning greedy persons,' says Carlyle, ' are to be found in every age. The question always remains, Did they lie chained, subordinate in this world's business . . . a true never-ending attempt going on to handcuff, to silence and suppress them ? Or did they walk openly abroad, the envy of a general valet-population, and bear sway ; professing without universal anathema, almost with general assent, that they were the Orthodox Party, that they, even they, were such men as you had a right to look for ? '[1]

1 **Everything that contaminates either flesh or spirit.** As a rule, Paul uses the term ' flesh ' to denote the human personality as enslaved to sin, ' the natural man ' ; while ' spirit ' is the Divine creative principle of the ' spiritual man,' or Christian. Here the terms are used in a non-technical sense, and are equivalent to our ' body and soul ' (cf. ii. 13 and vii. 5 in A.V.). **Let us be fully consecrated by reverence for God.** Here Paul strikes that Hebrew note of ' holiness ' (see A.V.) which reverberates throughout the Old Testament. To be ' holy ' or **consecrated** means that we belong to God. The moral demand of this relationship is determined by our conception of God, and the extent of our surrender to His will.

[1] *Oliver Cromwell*, Introduction, chapter **v.**

II. THE SEVERE LETTER
(x. 1–xiii. 10)

x. 1–6 : A DECLARATION OF WAR

x.

I appeal to you myself by the gentleness and consideration of 1
Christ—the Paul who is ' humble enough to your face
when he is with you, but outspoken enough when he gets
away from you.' I beg of you that when I do come I may 2
not have to speak out and be peremptory ; but my mind
is made up to tackle certain people who have made up
their minds that I move on the low level of the flesh. I 3
do live in the flesh, but I do not make war as the flesh
does ; the weapons of my warfare are not weapons of the 4
flesh, but divinely strong to demolish fortresses—I demolish 5
theories and any rampart thrown up to resist the knowledge of God, I take every project prisoner to make it obey
Christ, I am prepared to court-martial anyone who remains 6
insubordinate, once your submission is complete.

The arguments in favour of regarding chapters x. 1–xiii. 10
as part of an intermediate letter, written from Ephesus immediately after the ' painful visit ' referred to in ii. 1, are given
on pp. xvi. ff. These chapters are penned after Paul met a
complete defiance of his authority at Corinth, and after he
had experienced some gross insult. It is unfortunate that
the whole letter has not been preserved. Had the whole been
extant, we would have been better able to understand why
it was so effective in restoring order out of chaos, and in re-
establishing Paul's own authority. The letter could not have
been almost entirely taken up with self-defence and denunciation of opponents. **I appeal to you myself** need not be 1
taken to mean that Paul takes the pen from his amanuensis,
as in Gal. vi. 11. Here Paul uses the Greek first personal pro-
noun singular. In the great majority of cases where he uses
the plural, and the English versions translate ' we,' Paul is
also referring to himself alone, but is not calling attention to
his own state of mind or his own authority, as here.[1] **The**

[1] Cf. p. xxxv.

7

gentleness and consideration of Christ. Another rendering would be ' the meekness and reasonableness of Christ.' ' Meekness ' is the quality which Jesus claims for Himself in Matt. xi. 29, where Dr. Moffatt again translates ' gentle.' ' Meekness,' however, in the New Testament refers primarily to an attitude towards God. It is the sense of ' creatureliness.' ' It is He that hath made us and not we ourselves.' Trench has well defined meekness in the New Testament, in contrast with the Greek conception for which it is still constantly mistaken,[1] as ' the temper of spirit in which we accept God's dealings with us, without disputing or resisting.'[2] These dealings may be mediated to us through the unfriendly, selfish, or vindictive action of others. The idea of meekness in the Christian sense underlies Paul's words in Rom. xii. 19, ' Avenge not yourselves, but give place unto wrath ; for it is written, Vengeance belongeth unto Me ; I will recompense, saith the Lord.' The Johannine saying includes the content of ' meekness ' as applied to Jesus ; ' I am come not to do Mine own will, but the will of Him that sent Me.' When he invokes the ' meekness of Christ,' Paul seeks to begin by committing, as Christ did, his cause into the hands of God. He is deeply conscious that he is not merely engaged in self-defence, but is about to strike a blow in Christ's service. The ' meekness ' of which Paul speaks here is clearly the avoidance neither of controversy nor of forcible language and such forcible means to obtain obedience as was in his power (x. 3 f.). Gentleness seems hardly the appropriate word for such a context. The consideration of Christ. The ' moderation ' of Phil. iv. 5 (A.V.) is a rendering of the same idea, but this word in modern English either tends to mean lack of enthusiasm or confuses the passing of clear moral judgments with uncharitableness. The Greek word stands for a noble virtue which requires no re-minting. It denotes that legal rights towards others, and merely legal judgments of their conduct, must give way to

[1] Aristotle's idea of ' meekness ' was a certain equanimity of temper, which is angry ' only with the right persons, on the right occasions, and in the right manner.' It excludes irascibility, quick temper, sullenness, and implacability (*Nic. Ethics*, IV. xi.).

[2] *Synonyms of the New Testament*, p. 147.

a charitable insight into motives and circumstances. The *summum jus* must not ' in practice prove the *summa injuria.*'[1] A good example of the virtue is Paul's plea for the offender (ii. 6 ff.), where, having in the first place demanded that he be disciplined, he now virtually asks the community to practise **consideration,** lest the continued effect of their judgment may lead to ultimate loss of self-respect, or to moral deterioration, in the subject of it. **Consideration** in this sense corrects the deficiences of purely legal judgment, which is necessarily impersonal, applies to all alike, and can make no allowances. This quality, like ' meekness,' Paul sees embodied in the character of Jesus, and the fact is interesting as showing how it must have been his habit to instruct his converts regarding the spirit and example of Jesus. Bishop Paget has defined this **consideration** in a remarkable sermon on Luke ix. 56 : ' Giving people time ; not quickly taking them at their word ; not closing up the account, or forcing a complex matter to a speedy issue ; not insisting that men must mean all that their words, or even their deeds, imply ; making allowance for the different capacity, and form, and character, and move-ment of different minds ; remembering by what different avenues, and with what different stages and tokens of accept-ance, the same truth may be penetrating different hearts.'[2] Whether Paul is true to his ideal at all points or not, this spirit of Christlike ' meekness ' and ' consideration ' is the plane on which he would fain keep his thoughts and motives as he pro-ceeds to write the severe words that follow. The result showed that he did not entirely fail to do so. Clement of Rome well describes the same spirit : ' Let us make intercession for them that are in any transgression, that forbearance and humility may be given them, to the end that they may yield not unto us, but unto the will of God.'[3] Matthew Arnold's ' sweet reasonableness '[4] is a somewhat sugary designation but an essentially true description of Paul's conception.

[1] Trench, *op. cit.,* p. 148.
[2] *Studies in the Christian Character,* pp. 177 ff.
[3] *Epistle to the Corinthians,* § 56.
[4] *Literature and Dogma,* chapter iii.

Humble enough to your face (see Introduction, p. xxxii.).
2-3 **Moving on the low level of the flesh**—i.e. untrustworthy,
tortuous, cowardly, and, at a safe distance, a bully. We
must remember that Paul uses the term **flesh** in two senses.
It may either mean human life and its conditions generally, or it more often has a technical sense—human nature
as dominated by those lower motives which take possession
of the human heart when left to itself. The latter is what
Paul calls **your weak nature** (Rom. vi. 19), or **sinful flesh**
(Rom. viii. 3). Three times in this letter (ii. 13, vii. 1, 5)
Paul uses the term ' flesh ' and ' spirit ' in a non-technical,
popular sense, meaning just what we mean by 'body' and
' soul.' These usages must not be pressed in order to assert
that Paul held gnostic views, which distinguished ' flesh ' as
a grosser form of existence which must be got rid of ere the
' spirit ' could be free. That Paul uses the terms both in a
popular and in a technical sense means only that ' language
is made for man : not man for language ' (Plummer). The
technical sense of ' spirit ' in Paul is the Divine Spirit of Christ,
which takes possession of the natural man, and enables him
to become ' spiritual '—in other words, a Christian in heart
and in life.

4-6 The military metaphors are well brought out in Dr. Moffatt's
translation. It would be an entire misunderstanding to say
that, in thus opposing **theories**, Paul is condemning the use
of the human reason. The word might be rendered ' sophis-
tries.' As Denney pertinently says, ' Nobody but an evangelist
could have written this sentence. Paul knew from experience
that men fortify themselves against God : they try to find
impregnable positions in which they may defy Him, and live
their own life.' Had he not done so himself, when he framed
the ' theory ' that a Man on a Cross could not be the Messiah ?
Paul also knew, from the manner in which he himself, holding
such a theory and with **weapons of the flesh** in his hands, had
been overthrown by God, that no such weapons could be of any
avail. It is not human reason, but its abdication in favour
of prejudice, that Paul opposes. The **knowledge of God** is,
of course, the revelation made in Jesus Christ (cf. notes on

iv. 6).[1] They are not chiefly the attempts to disprove it, but to offer moral resistance to it, of which Paul is thinking. Yet the theories and any rampart thrown up to resist the knowledge of God are broadly enough conceived so as to range from the flimsiest excuses made to hide the effect of the Christian appeal, to conceptions of the universe and of human nature, which ' leave out the most obvious realities.' ' Rationalizing,' in the sense of modern psychology, may be the source of such theories, and the best psychologists are aware of the fact. ' A rationalization may be defined as a chain of argument used by the mind to justify itself in the holding of a belief which really owes its origin to something else—to suggestion or to some *affective* root.'[2] Paul's opponents are ' rationalists ' in this sense. The ' affective ' or emotional root of their opposition, where it is not malice or spiritual pride, is an inherited prejudice in favour of Christianity regarded as a continuation and improvement of Judaism.

Paul seeks to take every project prisoner to make it obey Christ. The word translated project may be used in a good or in a bad sense. It is the same as thoughts (Phil. iv. 7) and manœuvres (ii. 11). The reason why projects need guarding, and divinely strong weapons alone can capture or demolish them, is that Paul is remembering that man-made enterprises, even for the purpose of defending the right, may easily become subject to the manœuvres of the spirit of evil. He includes his own projects as well. Paul was accustomed to seek Divine guidance, and, as the account of him in Acts shows, often received it. Yet even when the ' visions ' he had and the voices he heard were accompanied by evidently supernatural features, he tested them. ' A man who has visions from one side will have them from the other ; if he has guidance, if he is " told what thou must do," he is open to misleading too ; there will be " messengers of Satan." '[3] We may further note the place which he gives to ecstatic visions in his religious experience (xii. 1 ff.).

[1] Cf. pp. 19 ff.
[2] R. H. Thouless, *Introduction to the Psychology of Religion*, p. 81.
[3] T. R. Glover, *Paul of Tarsus*, p. 189.

There is no doubt that the translations of A.V. ('revenge') and R.V. ('avenge') are both unsuitable. The word means 'bring to justice,' but it may be questioned whether Dr. Moffatt's **court-martial** does not extend the series of military metaphor unduly. There is no ground for assuming that Paul's meaning is that any recalcitrants who may remain, after the submission is complete of the rest of the community, will be brought before a court of the Church. Probably all that Paul means is that he will continue to maintain discipline and himself bring to book anyone who **remains insubordinate.**

x. 7–18 : Authorized Boasting

x.

7 Look at this obvious fact. So-and-so is perfectly sure he 'belongs to Christ'? Well then, let him understand, on second thoughts, that I 'belong to Christ' as much as he

8 does. Even supposing I were to boast somewhat freely of my authority (and the Lord gave it to me for building you up, not for demolishing you), I would feel quite justified.

9 But I am not going to seem as if I were 'overawing you

10 with a letter,' so to speak. My opponent says, 'Paul's letters are weighty and telling, but his personality is weak

11 and his delivery is beneath contempt.' Let him understand that I will act when I arrive, as forcibly as I express

12 myself by letter when I am absent. I do not venture to class myself or to compare myself with certain exalted individuals ! They belong to the class of self-praisers ; while I limit myself to my own sphere,* I compare myself

13 with my own standard, and so my boasting never goes beyond the limit—it is determined by the limits of the sphere marked out for me by God. That sphere stretches

14 to include yourselves ; I am not overstepping the limit, as if you lay beyond my sphere ; I was the very first to

15 reach you with the gospel of Christ. I do not boast beyond my limits in a sphere where other men have done the work ; my hope rather is that the growth of your faith will allow

* Omitting οὐ συνιοῦσιν · ἡμεῖς δὲ with D*, etc.

me to enlarge the range of my appointed sphere and preach 16
the gospel in the lands that lie beyond you, instead of boasting within another's province over work that is already
done. However, *let him who boasts boast of the Lord* ; for 17·
it is not the self-praiser with his own recommendations 18
who is accepted, it is the man whom the Lord recommends.

This whole passage is full of grammatical difficulties. Indeed, there are moments when the grammar breaks down
altogether, and the meaning can only be conjectured. This
is specially true of verses 12–18. If Paul actually spoke, sometimes, as he writes, it is no wonder that his opponents said
that his speaking was ' of no account ' (verse 10) and did not
come up to the standards of Greek oratory ! The difficulties
are reflected in the A.V. and R.V. renderings.

Look at this obvious fact (*lit.*, ' the things that are before 7
your face '). Note the imperative mood, as against the A.V.
and R.V. Certain facts that lay on the very surface of their
case discredit Paul's opponents and accredit him. (Both ' Ye
look ' [R.V.] and ' Do ye look ? ' [A.V., R.V. margin] are
grammatically possible, and would imply that Paul blames
his readers for not looking below the surface, and accepting
at their face value the claims and statements of his opponents.)
So-and-so does not imply that Paul is thinking of any particular individual, but of a particular type of man who claims
to stand in a special relation to Christ. **He is perfectly sure**
(*lit.*, ' sure in his own mind '). But such a man should see the
obvious fact, which does not exist merely in Paul's imagination, or anyone else's, that **Paul belongs to Christ.** By this is 8
meant his claim to the apostolic office, which is accompanied
by all the outward signs of an apostle (cf. xi. 23 ff., xii. 12).
Indeed, he might use stronger language about his **authority.**
He restrains himself, however. That **authority was given
me for building you up, not for demolishing you.** There may
be an ironical reference to the destructive influence these
spurious apostles (xi. 13) had exercised on the community.
The situation was not what they contemplated, and was 9
beyond their control (p. xxvii.). This is followed by another

13

ironical touch. ' I remember,' he says, ' that I am writing a letter, and will be accused of **overawing you** ' (cf. x. 1). 10 Again, **my opponent** is not a reference to a particular individual. Paul returns again to the sneer, of which another version is given in verse 1. ' Bodily presence ' (A.V.) is a literal translation of the Greek, but has led to misunderstanding. The scoff is directed not merely at Paul's physical appearance, but at **his personality.** The effort he made at Corinth when he tried to speak is said to be **weak,** ineffective. It is doubtful whether **delivery** completely expresses the meaning. The **delivery** was part of the ineffectiveness, but probably the Greek word *logos* denotes his message and its content. This ' ineffectiveness ' is set in sharp contrast with the impression produced by the letters, which are said to be **weighty and telling.** (Perhaps ' imposing ' would be a more suitable word than **telling.**) The scoffer has in mind Paul's unwarranted assumption of apostolic authority. He ' lords it ' over men's faith (i. 24). Reference also is no doubt intended to the tone in which Paul often reproves his readers, and calls for moral obedience.

If we are rightly to understand the truth that underlies this charge of utter ineffectiveness we must turn to 1 Cor. ii. 1–5, and to the description there given of the beginning of Paul's ministry in Corinth. He says that before he came to Corinth, and as a consequence, no doubt, of the failure of his mission at Athens, where he made the attempt to meet philosophers and rhetoricians on their own ground (Acts xvii. 32–34), he **determined among you to be ignorant of everything except Jesus Christ, and Jesus Christ the crucified.** His preaching in Corinth **did not rest on the plausible arguments** of Greek philosophy, but **on the proof supplied by the Spirit and its power.** Paul confesses that he faced the situation in Corinth, where, as in Athens, among all classes of the population, philosophic ability and rhetorical skill were held in the highest repute, **in weakness and fear and with great trembling.** Thus Paul's very real distrust of his own powers, in his first appearance at Corinth, is described by the sneering tongues of his opponents as ' weakness ' or ' ineffectiveness.'

14

It is best to leave generalizations about Paul's preaching style—no doubt, like most men's, never uniform and often determined by the mood within—to his enemies. We have no ground for drawing from these disparaging words any generalization as to his eloquence, or want of it. On the occasion of his first visit to Corinth he was without that outward assurance with which an effective speaker usually meets his audience. Indeed, he seems to have been ultimately reduced to silence and violent gestures of protest, by a Jewish section of his audience (Acts xviii. 6). Yet his visit was by no means unsuccessful, as the existence of a Church at Corinth shows. How the thwarted missionary was enabled to draw, as often before, on the inexhaustible source of **the Spirit and its power** (1 Cor. ii. 4), and Christ's 'strength' was 'made perfect in weakness,' is clearly indicated in Acts xviii. 9, 10. There the Lord spoke to him in a night vision, as he lay sleepless, in words that are reminiscent of the encouragement given to another great and often fearful prophet (Jer. i. 8, 9) : 'Have no fear, speak and do not be silent, for I am with you, and no one shall set on thee to harm thee : for I have much people in the city.' We may be sure that what Paul experienced on his first visit to the city was intensified on the occasion of the 'painful visit.' To his enemies, on that occasion, in still greater measure he would appear as an ineffective and negligible personality.

A serious textual and grammatical difficulty emerges in these 12-verses. The last two words of verse 12, translated 'are without 13 understanding' (R.V.), and the first two words of verse 13, 'But we,' are omitted in the important Western group of manuscripts. Dr. Moffatt's note shows that he accepts the omission, which certainly gives a clear meaning. Paul speaks ironically in the first part of verse 12. He has in mind the fact that these men have entered the sphere of work assigned to him, **marked out for me by God.** He, remaining within his own sphere, has no one else with whose work to make comparisons—unlike his opponents, who compare their work with his. He therefore says, again ironically, ' I have no one else with whom to compare myself. It is inevitable that

15

I compare myself with my own standard, and so my boasting never goes beyond the limit.

On the other hand, the words omitted in the Western text are included in many important manuscripts of the highest textual authority. Some copyist would have difficulty in realizing that Paul is speaking ironically, and would regard it as inappropriate that an apostle should speak of comparing himself with his own standard. He therefore inserted the words that are translated both in the A.V. and R.V. In accordance, therefore, with a well-known rule of textual criticism, the more difficult reading is preferred as original.

14-16   The reference of these verses is to the sectarian activities of Paul's opponents. He had broken the new ground. These ' sectarians ' had intruded themselves, and sought to boast of **work that is already done.**[1] He is scornful and resentful, all the more that he has in his heart the longing **to preach the gospel in the lands that lie beyond you.** The effect of their interference keeps him tied to Corinth for an apparently indefinite period. ' The regions beyond ' can only mean the extension of his work further into Europe. Incidentally, the words give an indication that x. 1–xiii. 10 are not, like i.–ix., written from Macedonia.

17-18   Paul hears in his own soul a note of warning from the ' word of God.' *Let him who boasts boast of the Lord* (cf. Jer. ix. 23, 24). Paul is always aware of the spiritual poison that lurks in an atmosphere of sectarian antagonism, and ' he sounds the retreat,' as Bengel puts it tersely. It is as though he said, ' After all, apostolic authority is not really safe in my hands. God's recommendation is the only mark of genuineness.' Paul boasts, not that he is an apostle, but that God had made him one.

[1] Paul, in thus describing the practice of his opponents, indirectly describes his own missionary policy. It is one ' which refuses to claim big things within another's province, and in reference to what has been already achieved by others,' a free rendering of verse 15*a*.

xi.

I wish you would put up with a little ' folly ' from me. Do put 1
up with me, for I feel a divine jealousy on your behalf ; 2
I betrothed you as a chaste maiden to present you to your
one husband Christ, but I am afraid of your thoughts get- 3
ting seduced from a single devotion to Christ, just as *the
serpent beguiled* Eve with his cunning. You put up with 4
it all right, when some interloper preaches a second Jesus
(not the Jesus I preached), or when you are treated to a
Spirit different from the Spirit you once received, and to
a different gospel from what I gave you ! Why not put
up with me ? I hold I am not one whit inferior to these 5
precious ' apostles ' ! I am no speaker, perhaps, but 6
knowledge I do possess ; I never failed to make myself
intelligible to you.

Paul, again in irony, assumes the garb of a ' fool ' who 1
loves to boast, a garb which he has stolen from his opponents.
I betrothed you. Two interpretations are possible. (1) Paul 2
thinks of himself as a parent who has arranged a marriage
for his daughter ; or (2) a still bolder thought : God created
Eve and brought her to Adam. Paul, by the Divine power
entrusted to him, brought this community into being and
betrothed it to Christ. The imagery is freely borrowed from
the Old Testament (Is. liv. 5, 6 ; Jer. iii. 1 ; Hos. ii. 19, 20)
(1 Cor. iv. 17). Paul speaks of his **divine jealousy** on their
behalf, probably in contrast with the sectarian zeal of his
opponents. He wishes to distinguish his ' folly,' in which
at the moment he is indulging, from the ' jealousy ' of a
man who fears his own power is on the wane. He dares to
say that his is the ' jealousy of God.' Denney aptly cites
Samuel Rutherford's words : ' Woods, trees, meadows, and
hills are my witnesses that I drew on a fair match betwixt
Christ and Anwoth.' Like Rutherford, only with far greater
restraint of language, Paul thinks of the ' marriage ' as taking
place at the Parousia—**to present you to your one husband** 3

Christ (cf. Rev. xxi. 9). There may be a reference to a rabbinical legend in *Haggadah* : that the serpent in the Eden story actually **seduced** Eve (cf. notes on verse 14). The opponents are doing the Devil's work (cf. xiii. 14), and are putting suspicions into the minds of the Corinthians, which will ultimately destroy **their single devotion to Christ.** Dr. Moffatt (like the A.V. against the R.V.) rightly treats ' and the purity ' as a gloss.

4 This verse, as translated in the A.V., implies that the suppositions made are not true but imaginary, implying that no one could have been able to add anything to Paul's gospel. This interpretation, by which Paul appears to make a series of imaginary suppositions, must be rejected. Paul's fears are not imaginary. He is not likely to cherish real fears on the ground of imaginary suppositions. Dr. Moffatt's rendering rightly assumes that the suppositions are facts. **You put up with it all right when some interloper preaches a second Jesus** is transferred to the beginning of the sentence, and is substituted for the A.V. rendering, ' Ye do well to bear with him.' The words are thus more clearly seen to be sarcastic. **Why not put up with me ?** has nothing to correspond in the Greek, but represents the unspoken thought in the apostle's mind.

5 **These 'precious apostles.'** The rendering ' the very chiefest apostles' (A.V. and R.V. margin, ' those pre-eminent apostles ') is unfortunate. Paul is not referring to the Jerusalem apostles, Peter, James, and John, but to men who claimed to be their agents. A possible translation is ' these super-apostles ' (cf. xii. 11). The opponents apparently claimed to have the authority of the Jerusalem apostles behind them against Paul, who, they claimed, had no such authority. The word trans-

6 lated **no speaker** might be rendered ' layman in speech.' To this ' layman,' so called, has been entrusted the **knowledge** or gospel of Christ. ' In spite of my defects of utterance and imperfect " technique," you always knew what I meant.' The last clause of the verse is grammatically very obscure, and the text uncertain. Paradoxically enough, the best sense obtainable seems to be Dr. Moffatt's rendering, **I never failed to make myself intelligible to you !**

THE KNOWLEDGE OF GOD

Paul uses the word here, as elsewhere, in a semi-technical sense (*gnōsis*). It is practically synonymous with the Christian gospel. He speaks of this **knowledge** as the illumination which came to him at the moment of his conversion, in order that he might **illuminate men with the knowledge of God's glory in the face of Christ** (iv. 6). That the word is also used for what we would call ' experience ' of God, as a result of the gospel, is plain from various passages in the Corinthian .letters and elsewhere (1 Cor. i. 5, viii. 1, 7, 10, 11 ; 2 Cor. ii. 14, etc.). The usage is the same as when the Old Testament prophets speak of ' knowing God ' or the ' knowledge ' of God (Hos. ii. 20). This ' knowledge ' is not the result of a process of thinking but is initiated by God's own self-revelation to His people. He makes Himself ' known ' (Ps. xcviii. 2, ciii. 7 ; cf. Gal. iv. 9)—in other words, reveals His inner being and character. On the human side, this ' knowledge ' is personal communion with a ' living ' God ; a God whose will and activity are directed towards imparting to men, both in word and deed, an actual experience of Himself. Neither in Paul's writings nor in any other part of Scripture is attention seriously directed to the question whether there really is a personal God or not. All the emphasis is laid on the *knowability* of God. Paul's answer to the question of the knowability of God is contained in his *gnōsis*, or gospel, which was entrusted to him.

A certain religious significance would be attached to the word at once by Paul's Corinthian readers. *Gnōsis* ultimately gave the name to a body of heretical teaching within the Christian Church known as 'Gnosticism,' which appeared in developed form in the second century. But in Paul's day there was already an incipient gnosticism, very vague and flexible, which confronted him wherever he went on his mismisionary journeys, both outside and within the Church. Among the non-Christians it was a feature of that remarkable revival of religious interest which appeared everywhere in the

19

Roman world.[1] Men had become possessed with a common longing for personal ' salvation,' deliverance from the impact of those blind natural forces—war, earthquake, famine—which from time to time mutilated and destroyed human life. They were conscious of their helplessness, as subject to disease, and all kinds of danger.   There were demonic powers, 'gods many and lords many' (I Cor. viii. 5), who permitted these scourges to descend on defenceless men.   The individual was alone in such a dark and inscrutable universe, and craved for some kind of assurance that he did not merely inhabit a little space between the two eternities and then go out like a candle.   Men sought, therefore, to come into living touch with some god who was more powerful than these hostile powers, and was, as divine, an immortal being.   The incipient gnosticism which Paul met was an unsystematic and varied religious method, whereby men were enabled to hold communion with the ' Divine.'   The Greek conception of deity was a very fluid one.   Any 'god' would do; for it was chiefly an assurance of continued existence that was desired.   This religious method included the ' mystery-religions,' also unsystematized.   In these, mystic ecstasy was the chief instrument for attaining fellowship with, or getting to ' know,' the higher powers.   It is important, in view of much that has been written regarding the influence of the ' mystery-religions ' on Pauline and later New Testament thought, to remember that they were still religions and not one systematized religion, powerful enough to exert a creative influence on Christian thinking.

The 'mystery-religions' of the first century did exert a certain influence upon Christian communities, and Paul had to combat it.   His chief reason for antagonism is that the absolute and unshared position which the person of Jesus must occupy in the Christian religion was thereby endangered.   Paul is the pioneer of all those throughout the Christian centuries, including our own, who recognize that the Christian religion ultimately depends for its content, validity, and effectiveness upon its conception of the person

[1] See the fascinating chapter in *Roman Society* by Samuel Dill (III. ii.).

20

and work of Christ. Jesus' own question, 'Whom say ye that I am?' requires the answer which He, in His own mind, expected and longed for. That answer is one that lifts Him high—out of the ranks of ordinary humanity—in origin, self-consciousness, and achievement. Paul here, if anywhere, follows the mind of Jesus Himself.[1] **The single devotion to Christ,** which Paul feels is imperilled by the teaching of his opponents, raises no mere theological question. It is based on an experience or revealed **knowledge** of what Jesus Christ means to the Christian. This experience given him sets his mind working at that intellectual pressure so erroneously called 'mere theology.' Paul will not tolerate any religious teacher who takes on his lips the names, 'Jesus,' 'Spirit,' 'the gospel,' and means something other, and something less, than they mean on his own lips. God has revealed in Christ this 'knowledge' of Himself. The nature of the revelation determines the nature of the Christ who is the revealer. They are inseparable in New Testament thought. The gift of the knowledge of God without the Giver is bare.

xi. 7–15 : WHY WORK FOR NOTHING?

xi.

But perhaps I did wrong in taking a humble place that you 7 might have a high one—I mean, in preaching the gospel of God to you for nothing! I made a levy on other 8 churches, I took pay from them so as to minister to you ; even when I ran short, during my stay with you, I was no 9 encumbrance to anybody, for the brothers who came from Macedonia supplied my wants. Thus I kept myself, as I intend to keep myself, from being a burden to you in any

[1] The Marcan account, in particular, of the Great Confession at Caesarea Philippi shows that the belief was firmly rooted in the faith of the Christian Church that the mere acknowledgment of the Divine personality of Jesus by His disciples was insufficient, and indeed unfounded, without a recognition also of the Divine necessity of His sufferings, death, and resurrection (Mark viii. 27–33). It is expressly stated that a mere confession of Messiahship is not to be uttered. There is no reason to think that this passage owes anything to Pauline influence. It is fundamentally true to the self-consciousness of Jesus, and the primitive faith.

10 way. By the truth of Christ within me, I am going to make
this my pride and boast unchecked throughout the regions
11 of Achaia ! Why ? Because I do not love you ? God
12 knows I do. No, I intend to go on as I am doing, in order
to checkmate those who would fain make out that in the
apostolate of which they boast they work on the same terms
13 as I do. ' Apostles ' ? They are spurious apostles, false
workmen—they are masquerading as ' apostles of Christ.'
14 No wonder they do, for Satan himself masquerades as an
15 angel of light. So it is no surprise if his ministers also
masquerade as ministers of righteousness. Their doom
will answer to their deeds.

7 Perhaps I did wrong in taking a humble place. Searching
for any possible means of discrediting Paul's apostleship, his
adversaries had even made use of the fact that he would take
no money for his support from the Corinthian Church (cf.
1 Cor. ix. 14). On that account, they urged, he could not be
8- very sure of his apostolate. Made a levy and pay are both
10military words. Paul is engaged in a ' campaign ' (x. 3 ff.).
Mention of the generosity of the Macedonian Church reminds
us of Phil. iv. 10–20. There the warmth of his acknowledgment, the statement that he had been ' initiated ' into the
Divine secret of contentment, and the declaration that their
service to him was not to be measured by money, take on a
new reality if we realize that when Paul ran short in Corinth
or elsewhere, the shortage was due to his own renunciation of
monetary gifts, in order that his ministry might not be discredited (vi. 3). The relief that came at the moment it was
needed was the act of God. It was not the only occasion on
which Paul had experience of ' the particular providence of
God.' The words My God will supply all your own needs
(Phil. iv. 19) are the overflow of his own experience, and not
11 only at Corinth. His adversaries had insinuated that the
reason why he refused to take money from the Corinthian
was because he did not care sufficiently for them. It has to
be remembered that all the money received, both by Paul and
by his opponents, would be in the form of voluntary gifts.

In Greek circles, they are the sophists among the peripatetic philosophers who are condemned for exacting fees from their pupils. The genuine philosopher is supported by voluntary gifts : ' The practice of taking payment in advance is probably forced upon the sophists, as otherwise nobody would pay them a fee for the knowledge which they impart. . . . The value of philosophical teaching cannot be measured in money nor can an equivalent price be found for it. We must, I think, be content if here, as in the worship of the gods or the respect shown to parents, we make such return as is in our power.'[1] The relationship would be much the same between the Christian missionary peripatetic teacher and his converts. It was an age of travelling preachers and missionary philosophers.[2] To many Gentiles, Paul was one of a number. Elsewhere Paul recognizes the right of the Christian apostle to eat and drink at the expense of the churches (1 Cor. ix. 3 ff.). His refusal to do so created a situation all the more delicate and liable to be misunderstood in proportion as gifts of money from his Corinthian friends were spontaneously offered. To refuse such gifts might either hurt the givers, or, if they had allowed suspicions in their minds, give them cause to doubt Paul's valuation of his own message. We know that Paul worked in Corinth at his tentmaker's trade (Acts xviii. 3 ; cf. 1 Thess. ii. 9), in order that he might not be a burden on the community. Evidently, however, work of this kind either became scarce or was withheld from him in Corinth. He was sometimes in real need. Moreover, the practice of manual labour would probably be against him in a mixed Gentile community, where the healthy Jewish sentiment that the rabbi should also be one who could work with his hands for a living would be strange. To the Greek, that one like Paul should work with his hands would be degradation. In refusing monetary help, however, Paul also made use of a powerful weapon against his adversaries, inasmuch as they would feel constrained to imitate him in order to stand right with public opinion favourable to Paul. Paul says that he wishes to

[1] Aristotle, *Nic. Ethics*, IX. ii. (Welldon's translation).
[2] See S. Dill, *Roman Society from Nero to Marcus Aurelius*, pp. 334 ff.

12 checkmate them, and to counter their claim that as apostles they and he are working **on the same terms.**

13-
15
    Satan himself masquerades as an angel of light. The reference to Satan may be a reminiscence of a Jewish legend that Satan once took the form of an ' angel of light,' and joined the other angels in singing praises to God. Eve in the garden is said to have caught sight of him in this guise as he ' bent over the wall.'[1] Compare verse 3. Paul's point, however, is not that evil can be made attractive, but that it can actually be made to counterfeit goodness. These men **masquerade as ministers of righteousness.** Paul does not deny that his opponents are actuated by a concern for **righteousness** —i.e. for the doing of the Law. Yet this concern for righteousness is delusive. These men are not mere charlatans, but they are inspired by the wrong kind of spirit (cf. I John iv. 1–4). Satan himself has inspired them. The later Apologists for Christianity, confronted with resemblances between Christian and heathen religious thought and practice, did not in these see broken lights of the one true light, but regarded them as due to the deliberate imitation of demons, who are really the false heathen gods. The ' demons ' intended to present misleading and false fulfilments of the prophecies of the Old Testament. For example, Justin Martyr says of heathen writers that they are inspired by the ' demons,' and that ' when they learned that it had been foretold that He should heal every sickness, and raise the dead, they produced Aesculapius.'[2]

Apart altogether from his theory of Satanic inspiration, we must recognize that Paul goes to the root of the matter when he deals with the ' spirit ' that determines action and utterance, even in a good cause. Paul's opponents were neither unbelievers nor immoral. They were professing Christians, whom he roundly accuses of doing the Devil's work. In their desire to propagate their own opinions as to what was essential to the Christian faith, partisan feelings took possession of them.

---

[1] Strack-Billerbeck, *Kommentar zum N.T.*, III. 526.
[2] Cf. Kirsopp Lake, *The Earlier Epistles*, p. 221, n. 1 ; Justin Martyr, *Apology*, liv.–lxii.

24

They not only led others astray, but were themselves deluded. They did not recognize their own true motives, which might be personal vanity, bigotry, and racial prejudice. Paul asserts that these men are not conscious of the true source of their sleepless energy and tenacious conviction. A man may either defend orthodoxy or promote liberal views in the Church. In either case, his dominant motive, hidden from himself, may be a love of power, or concern for a party which is an expression 'of his larger self.' The result will be the rise of a spirit within the Church, alien to Christ's spirit, worthy of the severest condemnation. Their doom, says Paul, with characteristic vehemence, will answer to their deeds.[1]

xi. 16-21 : A Sarcastic Interlude by a ' Fool '

I repeat, no one is to think me a fool ; but even so, pray bear 16 with me, fool as I am, that I may have my little boast as well as others ! (What I am now going to say is not 17 inspired by the Lord : I am in the rôle of a ' fool,' now, on this business of boasting. Since many boast on the 18 score of the flesh, I will do the same.) You put up with 19 fools so readily, you who know so much ! You put up 20 with a man who assumes control of your souls, with a man who spends your money, with a man who dupes you, with a man who gives himself airs, with a man who flies in your face. I am quite ashamed to say I was not equal to that 21 sort of thing ! But let them vaunt as they please, I am equal to them (mind, this is the rôle of a fool !).

In the remainder of this chapter Paul at last enters into a detailed comparison of his own claims to be an apostle of Christ with those put forward by his opponents. Twice at least in the last two chapters he has approached the subject (x. 7, 8, xi. 1 ff.), turning aside from it with native reluctance to ' boast.' What I am now going to say is not inspired by 17 19 the Lord. These verses are partly ironical, and partly reveal

[1] See Denney's treatment of this passage in the *Expositors' Bible*, to which I am indebted.

Ec   25

Paul's passionate desire that anything he may say which seems to border on spiritual pride should not be mistaken for 20 an apostolic utterance. The charges here made against his opponents may well be true. These men did look on the Corinthians as converts to a cause rather than as fellow-members of Christ's Church. In their bigoted propaganda they would employ any means, short of physical violence, to win assent for their position. ' Devours ' (A.V.) really means **spends your money,** or alternatively, ' puts pressure on you to give money.' The strength of Paul's language may be accounted for by the fact that the Judaizers made demands on the Corinthian Christians to continue the annual contribution, which every adult Jew and Jewish proselyte was expected to make toward the support of the Temple at Jerusalem. It would be an additional grievance against Paul's teaching that it had either diminished or extinguished the sense of obligation to make this contribution.[1]

xi. 22–32 : THE MARKS OF THE LORD JESUS

22 Are they Hebrews ? so am I. Israelites ? so am I. Descended
23   from Abraham ? so am I. Ministers of Christ ? yes perhaps, but not as much as I am (I am mad to talk like this !), with all my labours, with all my lashes, with all my time in prison—a record longer far than theirs. I have been
24   often at the point of death ; five times have I got forty
25   lashes (all but one) from the Jews, three times I have been beaten by the Romans, once pelted with stones, three times shipwrecked, adrift at sea for a whole night and day ; I
26   have been often on my travels, I have been in danger from rivers and robbers, in danger from Jews and Gentiles, through dangers of town and of desert, through dangers
27   on the sea, through dangers among false brothers—through labour and hardship, through many a sleepless night, through hunger and thirst, starving many a time, cold
28   and ill-clad, and all the rest of it. And then there is the

---

[1] Cf. G. S. Duncan, *St. Paul's Ephesian Ministry*, pp. 42 f.

pressing business of each day, the care of all the Churches.
Who is weak, and I do not feel his weakness ?   Whose 29
faith is hurt, and I am not aglow with indignation ?   If 30
there is to be any boasting, I will boast of what I am weak
enough to suffer !   The God and Father of the Lord Jesus, 31
He who is blessed for ever, He knows I am telling the
truth !   (At Damascus the ethnarch of king Aretas had 32
patrols out in the city of the Damascenes to arrest me,
but I was lowered in a basket from a loophole in the wall,
and so managed to escape his clutches.)

The threefold **Hebrews, Israelites, descended from Abraham** 22
is a rhetorical description of the full-blooded Jew.   It is notice- 23
able that Paul qualifies his assent to his adversaries' claims to
be **ministers of Christ.   Yes, perhaps, but not as much as I am.**
The words in the translation—a record longer far than theirs—
have no equivalent in the Greek, and are intended to bring
out the sense of the Greek comparative (' more abundantly,'
A.V.).   But, in Greek usage, the comparative may really be
a superlative.   Paul means that his sufferings and hardships
give him a *pre-eminent* claim to be a **minister of Christ** (cf.
Matt. x. 24 f.).   It is unlikely that those men had endured hardships of this kind at all.   They based their apostolate on their
official relation to the Jerusalem Church.   Paul bases his on
his sufferings, and claims to be on surer ground than they.
The recital of hardships, perils, and persecutions is a commentary on his words, ' I bear in my body the marks of Jesus '
(Gal. vi. 17).   These marks are a sign of ownership, and may
well include scars and impairment of health (cf. also iv. 10).
The details recorded in verses 23–27 indicate how many experiences of this kind in Paul's life are unrecorded—indeed, had
none to record them, for he must often have suffered alone.
Here he wears his pains like decorations.   He is indeed not
only the minister but the slave (*doulos*) of the Lord (*Kyrios*),
the title for Christ which is most congenial to him.

Forty lashes (all but one).   The Law prescribed that **forty** 24
lashes may be inflicted on a criminal, but not more (Deut.
xxv. 3).   Hence the rabbinical prescription was thirty-nine,

27

in order to be on the safe side. The lashes would be inflicted by the synagogue authorities. They had the legal right thus to punish offending members of the Jewish religion, and evidently on these five occasions looked upon Paul as still a Jew who was bringing the Jewish religion into disrepute. Moreover, the converts he made would tend to raise awkward questions with the Roman authorities. Judaism was given a privileged position, and proselytising was not encouraged 25 among those who by birth belonged to another race. **Beaten** 28 **by the Romans**, i.e. with the lictor's rod. **The care of all the Churches.** It was while actually suffering physical pain, and in a condition of nervous exhaustion, that Paul often had to carry on, mostly by correspondence, the varied and exacting administrative work entailed by the needs and perplexities 31 of the communities he had founded. This Damascus episode is described in Acts ix. 25. Here it is introduced so abruptly that some scholars have suggested that it does not originally 32 belong to the text. The brackets in the translation indicate that the story is not connected with what precedes in verse 31. It is, however, quite possible to take verses 30–32 in close sequence. Probably a version of this incident had been circulated which was intended to bring the apostle into ridicule. The suggestion may have been made that he exaggerated the particular danger, that his life was not really imperilled, and 30 that he was guilty of cowardice. The words **I will boast of what I am weak enough to suffer** really refer to what follows. Paul gives his own version of what actually took place. The danger was very real, and God enabled his friends to deliver him from it. What to his detractors was a ludicrous situation, to him was a crowning instance of God's mercy. Hence his insistence on the truth of what he says in the impressive appeal to **the God and Father of the Lord Jesus, He who is blessed for ever.** Paul puts this Damascus episode last of all in the list of hardships, because never at any moment in his life did he feel so helpless and despairing. At the very beginning of his ministry, without that richer and fuller experience of God's providential care which he now possesses, from his present standpoint, the deliverance was all the more wonderful.

In the words of Calvin, 'this persecution was, as it were, Paul's first experience of active service '—*quasi primum tirocinium Pauli.* Then he was but a raw recruit in the missionary campaign. At that time the tale of that triumphant confidence, which is the theme of the great doxology, **If God is for us, who can be against us ?** (Rom. viii. 31 f.), was only beginning.

xii. 1–10 : Strength in Weakness

xii.

There is nothing to be gained by this sort of thing, but as I am 1 obliged to boast, I will go on to visions and revelations of the Lord. I know a man in Christ who fourteen years ago 2 was caught up to the third heaven. In the body or out of the body ? That I do not know : God knows. I simply 3 know that in the body or out of the body (God knows 4 which) this man was caught up to paradise and heard sacred secrets which no human lips can repeat. Of an 5 experience like that I am prepared to boast, but not of myself personally—not except as regards my weaknesses. (If I did care to boast of other things, I would be no ' fool,' 6 for I would have a true tale to tell ; however, I abstain from that—I want no one to take me for more than he can see in me or make out from me.) My wealth of 7 visions might have puffed me up, so I was given a thorn in the flesh, an angel of Satan to rack me and keep me from being puffed up ; three times over I prayed the Lord 8 to make it leave me, but He told me, ' It is enough for 9 you to have My grace : it is in weakness that [My] power is fully felt.' So I am proud to boast of all my weakness, and thus to have the power of Christ resting on my life. It makes me satisfied, for Christ's sake, with weakness, 10 insults, trouble, persecution, and calamity ; for I am strong just when I am weak.

Visions and revelations, and stories of translations to heaven, 1 are characteristic of later pre-Christian Jewish literature. These were not granted only to saints and heroes of the faith like Enoch and Elijah. Several rabbis are recorded to have had these experiences, and Paul may have brought over this type of piety from his rabbinical past. The existence of such a type of rabbinical religion is shown by the fact that his Jewish-Christian opponents also laid stress on ecstatic experiences as authenticating their teaching. Paul is reluctantly compelled to meet them on their own ground. He claims to have had such visions and revelations, as he claims to be able to speak with tongues (I Cor. xiv. 18). But Paul and his opponents attach different religious values to these experiences. To the latter they are spiritual accomplishments, giving their teaching an added authority. Paul does not make any claim to apostolic authority on such grounds. The 'signs of an apostle,' in his view, are the grace and power of God made manifest in his weaknesses. He has just given in the previous chapter an account of the kinds of hardship and peril from which God had given him deliverance. Now he begins to speak of another gift of God, his visions and revelations, of which he gives one example in verses 2–4. The meaning is not that they are of the Lord, as though he saw Jesus, but that they are granted by ' the Lord,' where ' Lord ' probably means God. They were momentary privileges given him by God Himself, but the ' glory ' attaching to them belongs to God 5 and not to himself. **Of an experience like that I am prepared to boast, but not of myself personally.** He regarded the rapture he describes as an abnormal experience, but nevertheless as a real God-given experience. It was an act of God's gracious favour towards him, with which he himself had nothing to do, and on which he dare not presume. Therefore, 2 he speaks of himself in the third person as **a man in Christ ;** in other words, 'a Christian man.' This ecstatic experience ' is not related like his other visions to his practical life; it stands alone, a form of the pure inner life of contemplation. Here we have the states and experiences from which he drew his strength, not for separate resolves, but for the certainty with which he proclaimed the higher heavenly world, and demanded devotion to it; that is to say, for the proclamation of the King-4 dom of God itself.'[1] **He heard sacred secrets which no human**

[1] C. Weizsäcker, *The Apostolic Age*, I. 371.

lips can repeat. What he heard was no part of the gospel committed to him, although the experience itself strengthened his own faith in the reality of God's love and favour towards him. We have no right to relate this passage with the **mysterious wisdom of God** referred to in 1 Cor. ii. 6, 7. Paul derives no esoteric doctrine from his visions. He knows that the deepest spiritual experiences are incommunicable. When he speaks of being caught up to the third heaven, or caught up to paradise, we need not enquire too closely into the celestial topography. The form of the vision is determined by rabbinical conceptions of God and the universe. Paradise was the blissful abode of the righteous after death, and was located variously in Hades, in heaven, and, more vaguely, ' above the earth.' Here Paul identifies it with the third heaven. The first chapter of Genesis and the vision of Ezekiel were each made the starting-point in rabbinical literature for a good deal of esoteric speculation on the structure of the universe and the mysteries of the Godhead.[1]

It is of interest to note that the whole tenor of Paul's thought here is against the notion that in a state of ecstasy the soul is actually nearer to God, or surer of God, than under normal waking conditions. This fact distinguishes his attitude from pagan conceptions of the ecstatic state, and also from that of Philo. Communion with God, for Paul, does not cease with the passing of the abnormal psychological condition. Philo, speaking of the ecstatic experience, says : ' When the inspiration has ceased and the excessive desire has relaxed, then [the soul] returns from Divine things, and becomes a man again, mixing with human affairs which were lying in wait on the threshold, only that they might lay hold of him as he emerged from the inner shrine.'[2] On the contrary, it is ' in the flesh,' and especially in the weakness and hardship incidental to the life he lived every day, that Paul experienced the power of Christ (cf. Gal. ii. 20).

The malady described as a **thorn in the flesh** cannot be identified with any certainty. Epilepsy has been suggested,

---

[1] Cf. G. F. Moore, *Judaism*, I., p. 411.
[2] *Concerning Dreams*, II. 233 (Yonge's translation).

31

with little probability. Other suggestions are some rheumatic or neuralgic affection, malaria, or ophthalmia. It is at least certain that the attack was accompanied by very severe pain, and was recurrent. A possible translation is ' a stake in the flesh.' The choice seems to be between a large and a comparatively small cause of bodily pain ; but Num. xxxiii. 55 may have suggested the expression. Paul probably refers to his trouble in Gal. iv. 13 f. ; but neither the reference there, nor the translation ' stake ' instead of ' thorn,' gives any clue to the nature of the malady. The pain evidently came on in severe bouts, which Paul describes as the work of an angel of Satan to rack me and keep me from being puffed up. Like many sufferers, as distinguished from spectators, Paul approaches the ' mystery of pain ' with utter simplicity. Pain is an evil thing, used by God for human discipline. There is no reason to conclude, as some commentators do, that the attacks occurred as part of the nervous reaction after an ecstatic experience. The religious value of this most intimate passage is not lessened by our ignorance of the actual malady. In a few direct and moving words, Paul describes how he was able to come to terms with his humiliating affliction, and become ' the happy warrior,'

> Who, doomed to go in company with pain,
> And fear, and bloodshed, miserable train !
> Turns his necessity to glorious gain.

8   **Three times over I prayed the Lord to make it leave me.** Paul knows the meaning of unanswered prayer, and also the ineradicable human shrinking from the humiliation of bodily pain. He also knows that a refusal may be an answer. He prayed to Christ, like a sick man in the Gospels, asking for healing. Christ Himself knew the discipline of unanswered prayer, both intercessory, in the treachery of Judas (Judas was chosen after prayer : Luke vi. 12 ff.), and personal, in Gethsemane. **He told me.** The answer, coming from such a source, is unquestionable. Dr. Moffatt brings out the finality conveyed by the Greek verb (' He hath said ' : R.V.). ' The answer is both continuous and final, present as well as past.'

Here Paul affectingly reveals the source of his Divine ' initiation ' (Phil. iv. 12) into the secret of contentment. The resultant mood is deeper than mere resignation. God's will is accepted as his own. His missionary work, so often hindered by bodily weakness, is secure ; it is enough for you to have My grace. His own soul also is at rest ; it is in weakness that [My] power is fully felt. The power of Christ, like the ancient *Shekinah* in the Temple, is resting on my life—both as it still touched and moved the lives of others and in the hidden depths of his own soul. Both without and within, Paul is

attired
With sudden brightness, like a man inspired.[1]

Note how the words of verse 9 shed light on the conception of grace. The ' grace of God ' may become a religious *cliché*, or at most signify ' a vague benignity.' Grace, here and always in the New Testament, indicates not only ' favour ' but power ; exerting its fullest power when human incapacity is at its meanest and weakest. The source of Paul's heroic energy and missionary fervour is found in the ' grace of God,' which is heavenly strength bestowed on men at those moments when they need it most, and can contribute none of their own.

xii. 11–13 : The Supernatural Powers of a ' Nobody '

Now this is playing the fool ! But you forced me to it, instead 11 of coming forward yourselves and vouching for me. That was what I deserved ; for, ' nobody ' as I am, I am not one whit inferior to these precious ' apostles.' You 12 had all the miracles that mark an apostle done for you fully and patiently—miracles, wonders, and deeds of power. Where were you inferior to the rest of the 13 Churches ?—unless in this, that your apostle did not choose to make himself a burden to you. Pray pardon me this terrible wrong !

The words instead of coming forward and vouching for me 11 are an additional indication that they were written before the

[1] Wordsworth, *Character of the Happy Warrior.*

words in iii. 2. Paul feels that the Corinthians have shown themselves ungrateful and disloyal to himself, inasmuch as they have left him to take the most distasteful course of defending himself. They might have been expected to undertake this defence. **These precious 'apostles'** refers to his Judaistic opponents. Another rendering is 'super-apostles,' which gives point to this final satirical thrust from a 'nobody.'

12 **Miracles, wonders, and deeds of power.** These cannot be classified and distinguished. They include, no doubt, healings, but chiefly spiritual results in the lives of his converts are meant. **Fully and patiently** paraphrases the Greek, which is literally ' with every kind of patience.' ' Patience ' here means endurance, an active, not merely a passive, virtue. The ' signs of an apostle ' (A.V.) were wrought, like the ' signs ' of his Master, under those conditions of discouragement which

13 are so fully reflected in this letter. **Pray pardon me this terrible wrong !** The irony is bitter. One of the deepest of all Paul's discouragements, and the hardest of his endurances, was the way in which his disinterested motive in taking no support from the Corinthians was distorted. Compare the notes on xi. 7 ff.

xii. 14–21 : NOT YOURS, BUT YOU

14 Here am I all ready to pay you my third visit. And I will not be a burden to you ; I want yourselves and not your money. Children have not to put money by for their parents ; that is what parents do for their children. And

15 for your souls I will gladly spend my all and be spent myself. Am I to be loved the less because I love you more than others ?

16 But let that pass, you say ; I was not a burden to you, no, but I was clever enough to dupe you with my tricks ? Was

17 I ? Did I make something out of you by any of my mes-

18 sengers ? I asked Titus to go, and with him I sent our brother. Titus did not make anything out of you, did he ? And did not I act in the same spirit as he did ? Did I not take the very same steps ?

You think all this time I am defending myself to you ? No, I 19
am speaking in Christ before the presence of God, and
speaking every word, beloved, in order to build you up.
For I am afraid I may perhaps come and find you are not 20
what I could wish, while you may find I am not what you
could wish ; I am afraid of finding quarrels, jealousy,
temper, rivalry, slanders, gossiping, arrogance, and disorder—afraid that when I come back to you, my God 21
may humiliate me before you, and I may have to mourn
for many who sinned some time ago and yet have never
repented of the impurity, the sexual vice, and the sensuality which they have practised.

Here am I all ready to pay you my third visit. See Dis- 14
cussion, pp. 63 f. A burden to you. Paul makes a far greater
demand than asking for money. He asks for themselves, their
submission to Christ, and their confidence in himself. Perhaps
Dr. Moffatt's rendering, children have not to put money by
for their parents, unduly limits the scope of the illustration.
The whole range and responsibility of parental love is in his
mind. His own love for the Corinthians has been anything
but clear gain. He has 'laid up' (cf. A.V.) for them a store
of spiritual treasure in his own ministry. At whatever cost
to myself, for your souls I will gladly spend my all and be 15
spent myself. The words are spoken in the spirit of Mark
x. 45. Compare the notes on verses 7–10. Another rendering
of verse 15b would be, ' Are you going to let your love diminish
as fast as mine increases ? '

The insinuation had been made that Paul was clever enough 16·
not to take any maintenance directly, but shared in the money 17
given to his agents.[1] Our brother refers to some unknown 18
individual whose character was so well known to the Corinthians that no question could be raised regarding his complete
honesty. His presence would guarantee Titus' integrity.
Titus was sent on more than one mission to Corinth, and is
himself the bearer of the ' severe letter.'

[1] Was any portion of the money collected set aside for the travel
expenses of the delegates to Jerusalem, of whom Paul was one, and was
this the basis of the insinuations ?

19 Mere self-defence will not clear the air of suspicion. Paul seeks to convince his readers that he is **speaking in Christ before the presence of God** ; in other words, as a Christian man who is not afraid to bring his conduct under the Divine scrutiny. **In order to build you up.** He is also concerned lest defamation of his own character should continue the work of disintegrating the Christian fellowship. His aim in self-defence is to build up a Church, not merely to refute slander.

20 He fears lest the relationship between them is not yet such as to make constructive work at Corinth possible. His judgment regarding the discipline that must still be exercised at Corinth, and their judgment of his own fitness to guide them in exer-

21 cising it, are still incompatible. Paul hesitates to return, lest he experience another humiliation. In I Corinthians, sexual vice is also rebuked. The Judaizing emissaries, no doubt unintentionally,[1] must have given fresh occasion and excuse to those who were still smarting under Paul's rebuke of their sensuality. A guilty conscience often cherishes resentment against whoever has brought the sin to light. Delay and hesitation in dealing with the ' incestuous person ' of I Corinthians must have poisoned the whole atmosphere of the Church, and encouraged moral laxity in other directions.

These verses 20-21 are the fullest description we have of the state of affairs that called for the ' painful letter.' We have a picture of a Christian congregation which contains men who have retained their worldly ambition, and have not been purged from motives of self-seeking. **Quarrels, jealousy, temper, rivalry, slanders, gossiping, arrogance, and disorder**—there is something strangely familiar in that catalogue. Paul's words, **I am afraid that my God may humiliate me before you,** will find an echo in the heart of every Christian pastor. When to these sins of selfishness and pride there are added sins of impurity, the humiliation is complete. Paul's heart was often lifted to heights of thanksgiving inasmuch as it had been made possible to found a Christian Church in such a typically pagan centre as Corinth. Yet he had his moments of humiliation. Is this the fruit of all his labour ? Let us not

[1] Introduction, p. xxvii.

forget that he also writes, **my God.** So far is he from seeing in this moral *débâcle* merely a personal injury to himself that he can discern the hand of God in it all. It is a personal discipline. Nowhere in this letter does the utter reality of Paul's personal religion shine through more clearly. He would not have feared to return to Corinth, and would not have had so **to mourn for many,** had he not been a profoundly Christian man, with the kind of love described in 1 Cor. xiii. burning at the very centre of his heart. Love of this quality increases men's sensitiveness to wrong, and lays on them burdens to which toleration or indifference are strangers. The famous Hymn of Love, ' if it is a rhapsody, is the rhapsody of an idealist who has come safely through contact with the disenchanting life of the Churches ; it is not a song in the air by one who idealizes religious life, but wrung from long intercourse with ordinary Christians, especially those at Corinth.'[1] Love is not one single emotion, but a whole system of emotions, manifested in behaviour in different situations.

> Love is joy and grief,
> And trembling doubt, and certain-sure belief,
> And fear, and hope, and longing unexpressed,
> In pain most human, and in rapture brief
> Almost Divine.[2]

xiii. 1-10 : THE FEARLESS SPOKESMAN OF A STRONG CHRIST
xiii.

This will be my third visit to you : *every case is to be decided on* 1 *the evidence of two or of three witnesses.* **I warned you** 2 **already, on my second visit, and I warn you now before I come, both you who sinned some time ago, and the rest of you as well, that I will spare no one if I come back. That will prove to you that I am indeed a spokesman** 3 **of Christ. It is no weak Christ you have to do with, but a Christ of power. For though He was crucified in His** 4 **weakness, He lives by the power of God ; and though I am weak as He was weak, you will find I am alive as He**

[1] J. Moffatt, *Love in the New Testament,* p. 182.
[2] H. Van Dyke, *Music :* ' The Symphony.'

37

5   is alive by the power of God. Put yourselves to the proof, not me ; test yourselves, to see if you are in the faith. Do you not understand that Jesus Christ is within you ?
6   Otherwise you must be failures. But I trust you will find
7   I am no failure, and I pray to God that you may not go wrong—not to prove I am a success, that is not the point, but that you should come right, even if I seemed to be a
8   failure. (Fail or succeed, I cannot work against the truth
9   but for it !) I am glad to be weak if you are strong ;
10 mend your ways, that is all I ask. I am writing thus to you in absence, so that when I do come I may not have to deal sharply with you ; I have the Lord's authority for that, but He gave it to me for building you up, not for demolishing you.

1   **My third visit.** See pp. 63 f. **Of two or of three witnesses.** This reference to Jewish legal procedure (Deut. xix. 15) must not be taken too literally, as though Paul intended to hold a judicial investigation on his return to Corinth. The chief offender was evidently dealt with later, by a Church tribunal, convened as a result of Paul's severe letter (ii. 6 ff.). Witnesses would be unnecessary, as his offence was known to all, and he had confessed his fault. The reference to the passage in Deuteronomy is characteristic of other citations from the Old Testament which Paul makes. It is due merely to an association of ideas in Paul's mind, and here is intentionally whim-
2-sical. He has already paid two visits, and on each occasion
3 has acted as **a spokesman of Christ.** This third visit will prove that he is indeed so (verse 3). The general tone of the passage, however, is stern, and conveys Paul's firm conviction that the risen Christ, speaking and working through His apostle, is stronger than the sins of His Church.
4   At the crucifixion, sin seemed victorious. It seemed to have its way with Christ **in His weakness.** Paul is weak, but only **as He was weak.** At the moment he seems powerless to deal with the rebellion at Corinth. He has been ' crucified with Christ,' but he has also ' risen with Christ.' He will come clothed with Christ's own power to deal with rebellious men.

Paul's doctrine of the Cross is no hard and fast, firmly enclosed, theological system. The aspect which meets us here must not be lost sight of. It was in a similar mood that an old Scottish preacher (the father of Dr. John Brown), once said, ' Where are now those men who crucified Christ ? They are either at Christ's feet or under them.' **Though I am weak as He was weak, you will find that I am alive as He is alive by the power of God**, is a convincing paraphrase of the Greek, which is more literally rendered in the A.V. Here Paul is thinking of the power with which he is invested as an apostle of the risen Christ. Then, as though to dispel from the minds of his readers any thought that he is speaking merely of his own disciplinary authority, Paul bids them realize anew their personal Christian faith. **Christ Jesus is within you.** The 5 same living power that was communicated to Paul, as in moments of discouragement he contemplated the victory of the Cross through weakness, may be theirs also. The word 6 translated **failure**, or ' reprobate ' (A.V.), means tried and tested by God, and rejected. **I am no failure.** When Paul thinks of himself as a possible **failure**, he is thinking of failure to convince the Corinthians of his own apostolic authority. The **failure** is failure to **prove to you that I am indeed a spokes-** 7 **man of Christ** (verse 3). Compare Rom. ix. 3. ' He is willing to let the proof of his own authority, and so of his own worthiness, remain in abeyance. He knows that he has the right and power to exercise discipline of the extremest kind, but he will sacrifice everything, even the knowledge that it is so, if only he can persuade the Corinthians to give him no occasion to apply it.'[1] There will be no need to apply it if they put themselves **to the proof,** and his hope and prayer in verses 6 f. are realized. Proof that Paul is a genuine apostle is less important than that the Corinthians should prove themselves genuine Christians.

I cannot work against the truth, but for it. This is not 8 equivalent to *magna est veritas et praevalebit*. Paul does not mean to say that it is impossible for anyone successfully to oppose the truth. The key to his words is found in verse 7.

[1] C. Anderson Scott, *Peake's Commentary.*

' I am not concerned chiefly to be found in the right,' he says,
' and that you should be found in the wrong. That would be
to introduce an element of personal satisfaction which would
be hostile to the truth (or the message entrusted to me).'
Thus the words are connected with the context both of the
preceding and following verse.

III. A LETTER FROM MACEDONIA
(i.–ix.)

i. 1–2 : THE APOSTOLIC SALUTATION

i.

1 Paul, an apostle of Christ Jesus by the will of God, and brother
    Timotheus, to the Church of God at Corinth as well as to

2   all the saints throughout the whole of Achaia : grace and
    peace to you from God our Father and the Lord Jesus
    Christ.

1   **Paul, an apostle of Christ Jesus by the will of God.** Paul
emphasizes that he has not usurped the office. The repudia-
tion of his credentials by his opponents in Corinth is the heart
of the controversy in chapters x.–xiii. 10. **By the will of God**
may be regarded as signifying that the battle is won, and that
he can once more rely on the acceptance of his claim in the
Corinthian Church. There is no reason at all to think that
in speaking of his colleague as **brother Timotheus** he is implicitly refusing to give him the title ' apostle.' ' Brother '
is the name for a member of the Christian fellowship. The
remarkable thing is that Timothy should here be mentioned
at all. There is reason to think that Timothy's mission to
Corinth (1 Cor. xvi. 10 f., Discussion, p. 68) had failed.
The failure was due partly to the extreme difficulty of the
situation with which he had to deal, and probably also to a
certain lack of courage and resource in Timothy's handling
of it. Paul introduces his name alongside his own because
he wishes that Timothy as well as himself should be rehabili-
tated in the eyes of the Corinthian Church. This reference to

Timothy is an example of Paul's unselfish and generous desire to smooth the path of his helpers.

WHO WERE THE 'APOSTLES'?

Quite clearly Paul does not confine the term to those who are known as ' The Twelve.' Silvanus and Timothy are both mentioned as ' apostles ' in 1 Thess. ii. 6—though **as apostles of Christ we had the power of claiming to be men of weight.** The names of Silvanus and Timothy stand along with Paul's at the head of the letter, and it is natural to include them under ' we.' Titus and another unnamed colleague of Paul's are called ' apostles of the Church ' in 2 Cor. viii. 23. The word is really equivalent to ' missionary.' In Herodotus (i. 21) it has the meaning of ' messenger ' or ' envoy.' Harnack has very much on his side when he argues that there existed a class of Jewish officials who were called 'apostles,' whose business it was to collect, from the Diaspora, contributions for the Temple and to keep the Churches in contact with Jerusalem and with one another. Paul himself may have been an ' apostle ' when he went with ' letters ' from ' the brethren ' at Jerusalem, on his campaign against the Christians in Damascus (Acts xxii. 5). It is unlikely that the name ' apostle,' which was undoubtedly used of certain Jewish officials in later times, was first borrowed from the Christian usage.[1] If that be so, the title (which is not denied them by Paul) might easily be borne by the Judaizing Christian emissaries who came to Corinth. Paul speaks of them as ' false apostles,' because, in spite of their credentials and their title, their message was false and its effects so disastrous. The fact that apostleship thus requires authentication is sufficient proof that Paul does not regard the title as confined to ' the Twelve.' Similarly these men contended that Paul was no properly accredited apostle and no apostle of Christ, because of the kind of message he preached. Paul insists that his apostleship is authoritative. The kind of authority he exercised, and of which he was so fully conscious, was not

[1] *Expansion of Christianity* (English translation, I. 409).

external, like theirs, nor externally conferred (ii. 20 f.). His was the authority of one who had been commissioned by the risen Christ, and who knew ' the mind of Christ ' (1 Cor. ii. 16). There are indications that Paul's controversy regarding his own apostleship may have caused a somewhat narrower defin-ition of the term to emerge. In Acts i. 21 f. the place of Judas can be filled only by one who had not only been present at the resurrection appearances, but had actually been a personal disciple of Jesus. Paul claimed that the latter qualifi-cation was not essential, and that he, as one who had also seen the risen Christ, had also a right to his place among those who were thus called to leadership in the Church. He derived his apostleship from the risen Christ Himself. The mention of an apostleship ' from men ' (Gal. i. 1) indicates that there were such ' apostles,' and that the name was not unknown in Jewish circles.

Paul, at least, attaches no narrow range of meaning to the term. His authority was further strengthened by his out-standing gift for administration, baptized into the service of the Church. The disciplinary power which he exercised in Corinth and elsewhere rested on no merely miraculous endow-ment, but was based on his unique relationship to the com-munity as its founder, and on his own Christian moral insight and moral courage. At the same time, the apostleship of those who had themselves companied with Jesus, and above all were ' witnesses ' of the resurrection (Acts ii. 22), was by that very fact unique. Paul also claimed his unique place among them as a witness of the resurrection (1 Cor. xv. 8 f.). Just because apostleship in this sense was unique, it is incommunicable.

1 Paul reminds the Corinthians that they are the Church of God. God Himself created the Church at Corinth. It is not merely a body of adherents to his own type of teaching, nor a voluntary association of people who hold the same religious views (cf. 1 Thess. ii. 14 ; 1 Cor. i. 2). His letter is addressed 2 to them as well as to all the saints throughout the whole of Achaia. Here Achaia means the district of which Corinth

was the centre; Christians at Cenchreae (Rom. xvi. 1) and Athens would be included. Saints (holy people) in the New Testament means 'those who belong to God.' In the New Testament the word never implies persons of perfect character, but those whom God, by the preaching of the gospel, has claimed for His own, and who have accepted the relationship, with its moral demands. 'Be ye holy, for I am holy' (1 Pet. i. 15 f.). The character of God determines the character of His worshippers. The greeting, **grace and peace to you from God our Father and the Lord Jesus Christ,** is to be understood as addressed to 'saints.' **The Lord Jesus Christ** has done for them what they could not do for themselves, and could not do without. He has brought **grace and peace.** The word *grace* signifies a gift conferred by God on man. It is an act of redeeming favour to the sinful and undeserving. It expresses a relationship due entirely to His initiative and eternal goodness, and is the source of all Christian achievement (cf. pp. 136 f.). Every time that Paul mentions the 'grace of God' we feel the heart-beat of the Christian message. *Peace* is not, in the first place, harmony between man and man, but 'peace'—or, to use Paul's great word, 'reconciliation'—with God (2 Cor. v. 19 f.). It means assurance and acceptance of the offered friendship of God, and faith that a God, of whom Jesus is the perfect likeness, is revealed in the life and death and resurrection of Jesus, forgives sin, and is in charge, not only of individual Christian lives, but of the world in which men live, with all its dangers, temptations, vicissitudes. This peace is more than tranquillity and ease of soul. It is the 'peace of God which passeth all understanding,' **that surpasses all our dreams** (Phil. iv. 7). It is not at the mercy of our moods or fears, but is God's historical revelation of Himself in Christ to which our only response is faith. *Peace* is the completion of the work of grace, and is itself a Divine gift.

Thus the beliefs that lie at the heart of the Christian message which Paul had brought to the Corinthian Church, are to him so real and vital that they emerge quite naturally. They re-mint the conventional epistolary greeting, found in contemporary letters. It is a remarkable fact that the Christian faith

43

thus made itself apparent in such a simple and common custom as letter-writing in that ancient world. Paul does not merely send ' many greetings and wishes for good health,' or hope that a friend may be enabled *gaudere et bene rem gerere*.[1] Hopes and longings now went deeper. Paul sometimes begins, sometimes ends his letters with a benediction. These are not instances of language suitable for a religious occasion, but a sign that ordinary human relationships had acquired new and eternal values, and that these mattered to God. Both *grace* and *peace* must be exercised between man and man if the experience of them as a Divine gift is genuine.

We may easily miss the wealth of Christian conviction which is gathered up into this opening salutation. Jesus is called **the Lord Jesus Christ.** ' Lord ' tends to become a lifeless term in our Christian vocabulary. When it is used in the New Testament it radiates an atmosphere of omnipotent love, where obedience and adoration are the appropriate human response. *Lord* is the same term that is used of Jehovah in the Greek version of the Old Testament, and represents the position, dignity, and authority which Christ has won in the hearts of these early believers, because of what God has done for them, through Him. Lord (*Kyrios*) is the ' name above every name,' and describes the relation of the risen Christ to mankind. The ' name ' is conferred by God Himself; for the initiative which enabled men to apply this title to Jesus was not man's, but God's (Phil. ii. 11). This linking together of God and Jesus by a single preposition—**from God our Father and the Lord Jesus Christ**—as the one source of **grace and peace** is not the result of abstract theological speculation, but of a real experience of redemption through Jesus Christ, of which God is the author. It is noteworthy that in verse 3 Christ is subordinate to God—**the God and Father of our Lord Jesus Christ.** God is the God of Jesus, and His Father.

[1] Horace, *Epistles*, I. viii.

i. 3–7 : SUFFERING AND COMFORT—A DOXOLOGY

Blessed be the God and Father of our Lord Jesus Christ, the 3
Father of tender mercies and the God of all comfort, who 4
comforts me in all my distress, so that I am able to comfort people who are in any distress by the comfort with
which I myself am comforted by God. For as the suffer- 5
ings of Christ are abundant in my case, so my comfort is
also abundant through Christ. If I am in distress, it is in 6
the interests of your comfort and salvation ; if I am comforted, it is in the interests of your comfort, which is
effective as it nerves you to endure the same sufferings as
I suffer myself. Hence my hope for you is well-founded, 7
since I know that as you share the sufferings you share the
comfort also.

The language of verses 3–7 is itself an argument in favour
of the view that chapters x.–xiii. 10 are part of an intermediate letter. The nervous strain and spiritual turmoil of
these chapters has here given place to a mood of thanksgiving.
The style of the whole paragraph lacks directness. The defect
is no doubt due to Paul's courteous desire to speak of the
' comfort ' which both he and they had received, without any
undue emphasis on the original situation.

Blessed be the God and Father of our Lord Jesus Christ. 3
Paul's thanksgiving instinctively includes, not only himself,
but his readers in one fellowship of praise (cf. verses 6, 7).
The A.V. wrongly separates **God** from **our Lord Jesus Christ**
(but not in xi. 31, Eph. i. 3, and 1 Pet. i. 3). **God** is the God
of Jesus. He has enabled us to think of God in terms of the
personal name **Father**. Though Paul regarded Christ as a
Divine Being, possessing **equality with God** (Phil. ii. 6), he
consistently recognizes the subordination of Christ to God
(1 Cor. xv. 24). The subordination is the same as we find in
the Fourth Gospel : ' I am come not to do Mine own will,
but the will of Him that sent Me ' (vi. 38 ; cf. v. 19, 30). Both
the Johannine writer and Paul recognize this subordination
as an eternal element in the relation between Christ and God.

45

Neither concerns himself with any theological problem that may arise. The term **Lord** as applied to Christ in the New Testament sums up the whole wealth of meaning which Christ had for the hearts and minds of His worshippers.[1]

5 **The sufferings of Christ are abundant in my case.** These are remarkable words. Paul's language is even more remarkable in Col. i. 24, which are rendered in the A.V., ' I rejoice in my sufferings for your sake, and fill up on my part that which is lacking of the afflictions of Christ in my flesh for His body's sake, which is the Church.'

In both these utterances Paul undoubtedly means to say this at least—that the flood of pain and sorrow which has so overwhelmed him is the same kind of flood that broke upon Jesus at the close of His ministry. These utterances should be taken along with his words in another part of this letter, where again he speaks of the strain and suffering involved by his work : **Wherever I go, I am being killed in the body as Jesus was** (iv. 10). Paul derives the deepest comfort from the thought, not only that Christ has endured what he himself is enduring, but also that it is in Christ's service that these sufferings are incurred. The simplest and most obvious interpretation both of Col. i. 24, already quoted, and of the phrase **the sufferings of Christ,** is that Paul is conscious of the honour done him, inasmuch as ' Christ the sinless Master should have *left* something for Paul the unworthy servant to suffer' (Lightfoot). We may also compare his words in Gal. vi. 17.

6 **The same sufferings as I suffer myself.** The Corinthians had been awakened by the ' severe letter ' (ii. 3 f.) to a sense of shame and remorse, and of the dishonour done to the fair name of the Church of Christ.

THE ' SUFFERINGS OF CHRIST '

Many of Paul's interpreters have taken the utterances of i.5 and Col. i. 24 to mean that in the misconceptions, slanders, and disloyalties which Paul experienced during the Corinthian revolt, Christ Himself was suffering in the person of

[1] Cf. notes on iii. 17 ff.

His servant. Underlying this interpretation there is a conception of the relation of the believer to Christ which is usually called ' mystical.' The believer and Christ are, as it were, one person. Christ *lives* in Paul. The believer is ' in Christ.' Dr. Moffatt's translation of Col. i. 24 introduces this idea of mystical union : **I would make up the full sum of all that Christ has to suffer in my person on behalf of the Church, His Body.**

(1) Paul is indeed capable of what may properly be called purely mystical or ecstatic experiences (xii. 1 ff.), but he never regards these as an essential part or source of the Christian message, or as normal Christian experience. This subject is more fully dealt with in the notes on xii. 1–5. The frequent Pauline formula, ' in Christ,' has been often interpreted in a ' mystical ' sense.[1] It is true that Paul's passion of love towards Jesus Christ is without parallel in the history of religious emotions, but the state of being ' in Christ ' is not exclusively an emotional condition. The love is evoked by the particular relationship described as being ' in Christ,' and does not determine it. In the origin of this relationship, God in Christ is the agent, and the idea is ultimately eschatological. To be ' in Christ ' is to be a partaker in the Kingdom or ' reign' of God, which is inaugurated and established by the death and resurrection of Jesus.[2] It is equivalent to the possession of the ' spirit of sonship.' Men are thus **heirs of God, heirs along with Christ** (Rom. viii. 17). Properly speaking, mysticism

[1] The use of the term ' mystical ' in English is ambiguous. Sometimes all that is meant is that religious convictions are reached, not by merely logical reasoning, or by the acceptance of tradition, but by direct intuition, as in the experience of conversion. In this sense it just means ' vital ' religion. The mystic proper has the definite sense that all intervening helps and channels to direct intercourse with God, like symbols and sacraments, or the worshipping community, are either of subordinate value or may be dispensed with. God is approached directly. The mystic has visions, in which he ' sees,' ' hears,' ' feels,' ultimate reality. He has a secret door, which God opens for him, into His presence. Paul's relationship to Christ is not that of the mystic proper. Christ is always the ' mediator.' He never becomes to him a ' principle,' and not a person. In other words, he always feels that his personality and Christ's are distinct. There is no mystical absorption the one in the other (cf. the notes on ii. 14).

[2] Cf. further on this subject pp. 113 f.

dispenses with a mediator. The human personality in the true mystic experience is absorbed in the Divine Being. The relation with God is not mediated, but immediate.

It is, I think, clear that no such mystical idea underlies Paul's words, the sufferings of Christ are abundant in my case. They can only mean that Paul has been compelled, by the torture and anxiety through which he has passed, to drain a full cup of that tribulation which Jesus promised to his followers : ' Ye shall indeed drink of the cup that I drink ' (Mark x. 39.). He is enduring the sufferings of Christ in full measure ; in other words, suffering foretold by Christ and incurred in the service of Christ. It is quite clear that only in this sense could the Corinthians be said to endure the same sufferings as I suffer myself. In repenting bitterly of their conduct towards himself, they became obedient to Christ, and bore the cost. They also suffered sympathetically with Paul himself, inasmuch as they realized that they had been the cause of his sorrow. The language of vii. 9–11 is very relevant here. When Paul thus speaks of his own sufferings as the sufferings of Christ, he has learned what he prayed to learn—to know Him in the power of His resurrection and the fellowship of His sufferings, with my nature transformed to die as He died (Phil. iii. 10). To these words verse 5 exactly corresponds : As the sufferings of Christ are abundant in my case, so my comfort is also abundant through Christ. The comfort is the experience of the power of the Risen Christ, transforming, as only the power of God can do, his sufferings into ' glorious gain.' Thus Christ lives, or exerts His power, in Paul. He describes the same experience in Phil. iv. 13: in Him who strengthens me I am able for anything. The notion that in Paul's sufferings Christ also suffers is entirely foreign to Paul's thought, here or elsewhere.

(2) By the sufferings of Christ, Paul means not only the endurance of persecution, but all that the struggle with sin cost him, both within and without. Paul does not hesitate to say that the agony of Gethsemane, as well as the agony of Calvary, may be reflected, however faintly, in the experience of every faithful servant of Christ. There is another utterance of

48

Paul's which is too exclusively considered in an abstract theological atmosphere, and regarded as Pauline mysticism. **I have been crucified with Christ, and it is no longer I who live, Christ lives in me** (Gal. iii. 20). On these words many passages in 2 Corinthians, and in particular those already quoted, are the best commentary. These words also were wrung from him in the midst of a fierce conflict for the truth. Paul was conscious of other factors than those theological ideas usually associated with his name, which gave Gethsemane and Calvary a living and abiding place in his Christian experience, and sustained his faith in the power of God which raised Christ from the dead.

(3) Even if we reject the mystical interpretation, Paul's language in 2 Cor. i. 5, interpreted as though it would set his own sufferings on the same plane with the suffering of Christ on the Cross, may still cause perplexity in the minds of those who are rightly accustomed to think of Paul as the exponent of a doctrine of the Cross whose content is that the suffering on the Cross is such as none other could have, or endure. If Paul's words here and in Col. i. 24 seem to endanger the absolute ' otherness,' the unique and solitary efficacy of the Cross as an act of God for man's redemption, Paul is evidently quite unconscious of the danger. It is he who also says, **Was it Paul who was crucified for you?** (1 Cor. i. 13). At the same time, Paul has no intention of regarding the suffering on Calvary as devoid of any point of contact with the human experience of martyrdom. Such a position would make the Cross unintelligible to any human heart which knows in itself the pain of bearing the sins of others, and the vicarious suffering which sin can inflict upon human devotion. The ' otherness ' of Christ's suffering on the Cross can only be apprehended by its likeness to Christian experience of suffering. Otherwise Christ's redemptive suffering is but ' a rock in the sky.'

The Cross of Christ, in one of those several aspects it presents in Paul's thinking, is a demonstration of what sin can do to the love of God, and the extent to which human wrongdoing matters to God. In whatever fashion Paul speaks of the Cross, he never thinks of it in abstract theological terms. His every utterance on the subject has in the background, as the ultimate motive of his words, the thought of the death of Christ as an overwhelming demonstration of Divine love. The object on which his mind is fixed is not an abstract historical fact that Jesus died, but the spectacle of Jesus, whom he now worships as risen and exalted, as One who, out of love, suffered even such a death for his sake. That the risen Jesus thus suffered and died brought unspeakable comfort to Paul, as it has done to millions of his followers in the hour of trial. That this same Jesus bade His followers take up the cross and follow Him has been their strength and inspiration in many a dark, lonely, and agonizing hour. It was the strength and inspiration of Paul. Yet no one who reads without prejudice Rom. viii. 1–17, or v. 14–19 of the present Epistle, can be in doubt either of the unique redemptive value which the Cross had in Paul's mind, or of the Godward direction in which the secret of that redemptive value lies.

At the same time, not on the suffering of Christ by itself, but on the person of Him who thus suffered at the hands of men, does the emphasis lie. It is not so much on Jesus' death Paul thinks as on Jesus dying. Difficulties about the atonement always ultimately resolve themselves into difficulties regarding the person of Christ. **For our sakes He made Him to be sin who Himself knew nothing of sin** (v. 21). The suffering of one ' who knew no sin,' and yet suffered in silence, without complaint, must be itself unique. Paul does not suggest that the experience of martyrs and confessors, least of all his own experience, is the key to the redemptive meaning of Calvary. Rather does the suffering of Christ, the Son of God, on the cross provide both a means of deliverance from sin and of encouragement and victory for those who suffer in Christ's service, and with a love like His in their hearts. The Cross of Christ, for Paul, is both an apocalypse of Divine redemptive love and a beacon to all who suffer ' according to the will of God.' James Hinton, in *The Mystery of Pain*, says : ' There are materials within us for an entire inversion of our attitude towards pain. The world in this respect, we might almost

feel, seems to tremble on the balance. A touch might trans-
form it wholly. One flash of light from the Unseen, one word
spoken by God, might suffice to make the dark places bright,
and wrap the sorrow-stricken heart of man in the wonder of
an unutterable glory.' To Paul the sufferer, the light came
in the sufferings of Jesus, though the word spoken was actually
a silence. Jesus made no remonstrance or complaint while
men tortured Him, because He knew, and therefore Paul
knew, that suffering of this kind is not merely purposeless.
It belonged to the pain God is allowed to guide (vii. 10).

i. 8–11 : Despair a Divine Occasion

Now I would like you to know about the distress which befell 8
me in Asia, brothers. I was crushed, crushed far more
than I could stand, so much so that I despaired even of
life ; in fact I told myself it was the sentence of death. 9
But that was to make me rely not on myself but on the
God who raises the dead ; He rescued me from so terrible 10
a death, He rescues still, and I rely upon Him for the hope
that He will continue to rescue me. Let me have your 11
co-operation in prayer, so that many a soul may render
thanks to Him on my behalf for the boon which many
have been the means of Him bestowing on myself.

The distress which befell me in Asia. The way in which 8
the subject is introduced shows that the Corinthian Church
is not hearing of this incident for the first time. They already
knew something of what had happened, but not its full extent.
Can we identify it, or must we regard it as hidden among those
many hazards and perils to which Paul refers in 2 Cor. xi.
23 ff. ? Probably the latter. A reference to this severe peril
is sometimes seen in 1 Cor. xv. 32, where Paul refers to having
' fought with wild beasts ' at Ephesus. It is extremely unlikely that these words are to be taken literally, as though
Paul had either actually been thrown to the lions, or was in
grave danger of being condemned to the amphitheatre. His
Roman citizenship would have saved him from such a fate.

It is much more likely that the 'wild beasts' were men. Ignatius uses the same word in that sense (Rom. v. 5). It is quite possible that **Asia** means Ephesus, where Paul had 'many adversaries' (I Cor. xvi. 9). Some have thought that the reference is to the riot described in Acts xix. 21 ff., and that Paul did not escape from it quite so easily as Luke's description implies. But that event had happened at least two years before, and the reference here is to some quite recent experience. What we know of the Ephesus riot from Luke's account does not in itself warrant the description of the desperate situation in verses 8–10. There may have been in Ephesus a subsequent plot against Paul's life, of which we have no record. The incident mentioned here apparently took place about the same time as the revolt broke out at Corinth. The mention of it would bring home to the Corinthians the fact that their disloyalty was not the only contributing factor towards his state of mind when he wrote the severe letter.

Whatever happened, Paul's language clearly shows that he suffered serious physical violence. Some attempt at lynching by the populace is suggested. **I was crushed, crushed far more than I could stand, so much so that I despaired even of life.** Paul is extremely frank about his mood in this peril. The gravity of the danger, and the hopelessness into which he fell, only enhance the marvel 9 of his deliverance. He seemed to hear **God Himself** pronounce the **sentence of death.** Instead, the experience gave him a fresh conviction of the power of **God who raises the dead.** Here Paul is probably quoting from a prayer which every pious Jew was in the habit of repeating thrice daily : ' Thou art almighty for ever, O Lord, for Thou makest the dead to live. Thou art mighty to help, Thou who sustainest the living through Thy mercy, and makest the dead to live through Thy compassion. . . . Who is like unto Thee, O King, who killest and makest alive and causest help to spring up ? And true art Thou in making the dead to live.' The words may well have sprung to Paul's lips when deliverance came from so terrible a death.

10 **He rescues still, and I rely upon Him for the hope that**

He will continue to rescue me. Such emergencies and dangers
are not over. He therefore seeks for the **co-operation in** 11
prayer of his Corinthian friends, in order that, if a similar
emergency occurs, he may have the powerful aid of their intercession, that he may again rely **on the God who raises the
dead.**

Saintliness did not come easily to Paul. ' The principalities
and powers showed no signs of allowing a victory without
dust ' (T. R. Glover). He has to do battle continuously with
weakness and temptation, with the burden laid on him by
' the care of all the Churches,' with personal discomfort, priva-
tion, and danger, with restlessness and despair. These are
the occasions when he lays stress, not on his own victory, but
on the victory of God wrought in himself. **I am proud to
boast of all my weakness and thus to have the power of God
resting on my life** (xii. 9). **We are more than conquerors
through Him who loved us** (Rom. viii. 37). Moreover, his
deliverances are not merely a private **boon,** but given in
order to equip him for service and to enrich the life of the
whole Church ; **so that many a soul may render thanks to
Him on my behalf.**

i. 12–22 : The Divine ' Yes ' and the Human ' Amen '

My proud boast is the testimony of my conscience that holiness 12
**and godly sincerity, not worldly cunning, but the grace of
God, have marked my conduct in the outside world and
in particular my relations with you. You don't have to** 13
**read between the lines of my letters ; you can understand
them. Yes, I trust you will understand the full meaning
of my letters as you have partly understood the meaning** 14
**of my life, namely that I am your source of pride (as you
are mine) on the Day of our Lord Jesus. Relying on this** 15
**I meant to visit you first, to let you have a double delight ;
I intended to take you on my way to Macedonia, and to visit** 16
**you again on my way back from Macedonia, so as to be
sped by you on my journey to Judaea. Such was my** 17
intention. Now, have I shown myself ' fickle ' ? When I

53

18
19
20
21
22

propose some plan, do I propose it in a worldly way, ready
to mean 'no' as well as 'yes'? By the good faith of
God, my word to you was not 'yes and no'; for the Son
of God, Jesus Christ, who was proclaimed among you by
us (by myself and Silvanus and Timotheus) was not 'yes
and no'—the Divine 'yes' has at last sounded in Him,
for in Him is the 'yes' that affirms all the promises of God.
Hence it is through Him that we affirm our 'amen' in
worship, to the glory of God. And it is God who confirms
me along with you in Christ, who consecrated me, who
stamped me with his seal, and gave me the Spirit as a
pledge in my heart.

12   Dr. Moffatt's rendering, holiness, is based upon a reading,
hagiotēs. Another quite well-authenticated reading is *haplotēs*,
'singleness of aim' or 'disinterestedness' ('simplicity,' A.V.).
On the whole the latter reading is to be preferred. The word
hagiotēs is not found elsewhere in Paul's letters. Paul says
that his relations with the Corinthians have been characterized
by 'singleness of aim' and godly sincerity, not worldly cunning but the grace of God. The Greek word for sincerity means
'examined by the light of the sun' and found pure. The
grace of God means much more than 'benignity' or 'kindli-
ness,' as always in the New Testament. It means here that
Paul's ministry has been entrusted to him as a special favour
by God. It would therefore be a breach of trust to use worldly
cunning: in other words, determine his plans and movements
by his own interests.

13-
16   There is no ambiguity about his life. The meaning both
of what he does and of what he writes is discovered in that
atmosphere of 'single-minded devotion' and godly sincerity
of which he has just spoken. The light that falls upon his
life is the testing and penetrating light of God's presence. It
is the same light that will fall upon every man's life—theirs
and his—on the judgment day, the Day of our Lord Jesus
(cf. verse 23). 'No one will rejoice then . . . that he has discovered the infirmities of preachers, or set the saints at
variance; the joy will be for those who have loved and trusted

each other, who have borne each other's faults and laboured for their healing, who have believed all things, hoped all things, endured all things, rather than be parted from one another by any failure of love ' (Denney).

Paul is accused of being **fickle.** The words **ready to mean** 17 **' no ' as well as ' yes '** do not entirely convey the full accusation made against Paul. The accusation of ' fickleness ' means also that he is considered to sit rather lightly to the affairs of the Corinthian Church (cf. p. 64). During the painful visit, before he left Corinth, forcible words must have fallen from his lips. He had said that he would return, and would **spare no one** (xiii. 2). Second thoughts had determined him not to pay what might be another painful visit.[1] The Corinthians did not understand why he should still wait until the Macedonian tour was completed, especially as they had done all that he demanded of them.

Paul swiftly passes from reflections on himself to any pos- 18 sible reflection on the truth of his message. **My word to you was not ' yes ' and ' no '** ; **for the Son of God, Jesus Christ … was not ' yes and no. '** The utterance has only a slight connexion with his apology for a change of plan. It is one of Paul's ' illuminative irrelevances.'[2] Here the missionary speaks. Any criticism of his own conduct may have disastrous effects upon the work.

Out of this somewhat humiliating *apologia pro vita sua* there 19 bursts suddenly one of the great descriptions of the Christian gospel. However ambiguous man may be, the gospel is a mighty affirmation. **The Divine ' yes ' has at last sounded in Him, for in Him is the ' yes ' that affirms all the promises of God.** God keeps His promises, however Paul does not seem to have kept his. Doubtless he feels that his readers must ultimately know that the man who makes it his main interest in life to proclaim the good news of God who has kept and fulfilled all His promises, cannot fail himself ' to be changed into the same likeness.' No man can learn tortuous ways in

[1] pp. 62 ff.
[2] T. R. Glover, *Paul of Tarsus*, p. 190. Even Gal. vi. 14 was written ' by sheer accident.'

such a service. This kind of argument ' might be *repeated* by a hypocrite,' says Denney, ' but no hypocrite could ever have *invented* it.'

20   All the promises of God are, of course, in Paul's view, another name for the whole message of the Old Testament. The word is used by Paul to describe that remarkable and indeed unique general characteristic of Old Testament religion which emerges in the conviction, lying at its heart and largely the fruit of the ministry of the prophets, that God has a future good in store for His chosen people, and that it will be realized for those who have faith in God's faithful word. By the promises of God are meant, not merely individual utterances, but the whole significance of the history of Israel. Even the historical books of the Old Testament are essentially a prophetic interpretation of history.

CHRIST THE FULFILMENT OF THE ' PROMISES OF GOD '

In the great spiritual saga of Israel's ancestor, Abraham, he is the first recipient of the promise. Canaan, the land of promise, and the birth of a son and the prospect of a numerous posterity, are in the line of its fulfilment. In whatever form, however concrete and realistic, any particular promise was regarded as fulfilled, the essential meaning of the term promise was that the future of the nation, and its commanding place and mission among other nations, were believed to depend solely upon God, and upon God's purpose for the world. The supremacy and inviolability of God's purpose is well described in Jeremiah's words to the Babylonian exiles. Their Jewish citizenship is no more. Jeremiah even bids them to be loyal to the foreign power that holds them captive. Yet the purpose of God remains unchanged. ' For well do I know the thoughts that I think concerning you—thoughts of weal and not of ill—to give you a future of hope ' (Jer. xxix. 11).[1]   Much hard discipline, however, did not purge that

[1] Trans. by J. Skinner, *Prophecy and Religion*, p. 287.

future of hope altogether from political or materialistic elements. These grosser elements persisted, as the popular Messianic expectations in our Lord's time show ; but hymns like the *Benedictus* and the *Magnificat*, however much of their content they may owe to Christian piety, make it plain that there were circles of pious folk who looked for a more spiritual ' consolation of Isreal,' and a more purely religious fulfilment.

It should be noted that in the words, **in Him is the ' yes ' that affirms all the promises of God,** Paul utters a distinctive and unique Christian conception which is not contained in the religious hope of Judaism. Christianity made a new and original claim when it taught that all the promises of God were realized *in a single person.* It is no mere accident of history, the fruit of no mere peculiar fantasy of a Semitic people, who regarded themselves as special favourites of heaven—above all, no doctrine peculiar to Paul but shared by him with the primitive Church—that the Old Testament history is claimed by the New Testament Church as a divine revelation, preparatory to, and finding, its fulfilment in Jesus Christ.[1] The new thing in Christianity is the belief that the promises are fulfilled in one Person. This fulfilment in an historical Person has its origin in the Messianic self-consciousness of Jesus Himself (Luke iv. 22). He saw in the features of the promised Messiah His own face, and taught His disciples to see in His own person and ministry, and more particularly in His own death, the complete fulfilment of the ' promises of God,' which express His eternal purpose for the world. The Kingdom, or ' reign,' of God has arrived in His own person and ministry (Luke xi. 20). ' The Son of Man must suffer ' denotes a necessity which is the working of no impersonal fate, but is rooted in the eternal purpose of God (Mark xiv. 62 f.).

The truth of Paul's words, regarding Jesus Christ as the final and absolute affirmation of God's promise and purpose, is not affected by any detailed or apparently whimsical arguments which he or any other New Testament writer may employ in order to discover predictive ' proof-texts.' Collections

[1] Cf. A. E. J. Rawlinson, *The New Testament Doctrine of the Christ,* p. 17.

of these proof-texts, or *testimonia*, were no doubt made quite early, and Paul himself may have used such a collection. Some of the predictions are based on rabbinical interpretations, and not on the primary meaning of the passages (e.g. Matt. xii. 40 ; Acts ii. 25 ; Gal. iii. 16). Least of all is the truth of Paul's words about **the promises of God** affected by any merely rationalistic and modern insistence, which appears still in certain ways of interpreting the Old Testament— either that each individual promise in the Old Testament has already been fulfilled in Jesus Christ, or that some are still awaiting fulfilment. No truly Christian interpretation of prophecy has any right to regard its subject as the Jewish nation and its future (for example, its return to Palestine). The truth of Paul's words is based upon two fundamental historical facts. The first is that the religion of Judaism is the only religion, before the coming of Christ, at whose heart is an undying hope, and a hope which is based firmly on a faith in God's own righteous power and love. Paul himself isolates this unique prerogative of Israel : **theirs . . . is the promises** (Rom. ix. 4). The second is the universality of the Christian religion. The non-Jewish peoples have themselves fallen heir to this ' future of hope ' through the coming of Jesus Christ. Formerly they were **strangers to the covenants of the Promise, devoid of hope and God within the world** (Eph. ii. 12.). In 2 Cor. i. 19 f., almost in a parenthesis, Paul is making two great affirmations which sum up the Christian philosophy of history. They are as momentous to-day as in the first century A.D. In Christ, men have seen all that God can do, and all that He has promised to do. Also, there is no hope for any civilization apart from acceptance of the Person and obedience to the teaching of Jesus Christ. The real and only alternative to belief in the ' promises of God ' is a profound pessimism as to the future of civilization, and of the individual.

20 **Hence it is through Him that we affirm our ' amen ' in worship, to the glory of God.** Paul ends this sudden and characteristic outburst by giving us a swift cameo-like picture

of a Christian congregation at worship, uttering its ' amens ' and continually reaffirming its faith in the fulfilment of God's promises in Christ. The picture is meant to be a confirmation of the reality of the ' promises of God.' It is not only in life, but supremely in the act of worship, that Christian men can commend the Christian faith to their fellows. Following on 21- this, Paul also gives us a glimpse into his own heart, and reveals 22 the basis of his own Christian certainty. **It is God who confirms me along with you in Christ, who consecrated me, who stamped me with His seal, and gave me the Spirit as a pledge in my heart.** This certainty does not ultimately rest on something outside itself, which is no part of it, but related to it only as a column sticks to its base by the force of gravity. That is the characteristic of the religious experience which rests upon an infallible Book, or an infallible Church ; upon the conception of an omnipotent God who ' never leaves His own creatures to approach Him without hedging them in, so that only wilful blindness can miss finding Him.' Paul bases his certainty on the belief that there is a direct aggression of God upon the individual soul in Jesus Christ realized in history, and that he himself has experienced it. The seeds of religious certitude are a constituent and essential part of the individual experience itself.

Consecrated me refers particularly to Paul's own apostolic ministry. By means of it he possessed an authority with those to whom he was writing which was not imposed, but imposed itself. Of this authority Paul makes frequent use. That it is no mere religious tyranny, verse 24 shows. **Confirms, stamped me with His seal, pledge,** are all popular semi-legal terms, which would be familiar in the commercial life of Corinth. The word for ' confirm ' means a guarantee given by the vendor. Goods, or samples of goods, were ' sealed ' for security in transit. ' Pledge ' or ' earnest ' is a portion of the purchase-price received in advance and guaranteeing that more is due. The possession of the ' Spirit ' is a God-given experience of Christian men whereby, amid the apparently stronger sway of ' principalities and powers,' within and without, they are enabled to walk in inward peace

59

and security, as children in a father's house (Rom. viii. 15 f.). This ' Spirit ' is a pledge of the believer's acceptance at the Great Day. To possess the ' Spirit ' and to be ' in Christ ' are, for Paul, ideas practically synonymous. When God gives to a man the spirit of ' sonship,' which enables him in prayer to say to God, ' Abba ! Father ! ' he is not only a child, but an ' heir ' (Rom. viii. 16 f.), with an inheritance awaiting him. This ' Spirit ' is at once a religious fact and a profound ethical motive. The Spirit is the ' Holy Spirit,' God's own Spirit, guaranteeing a permanent relationship to God having permanent effects in conduct, not a temporary endowment.

In stamped me with His seal there may also be an allusion to Christian baptism. At a later period in the Christian Church the metaphor of ' sealing ' was often used for baptism. It is easy to understand why, in Paul's mind, the ' sealing,' or the baptismal rite, and the gift of the Spirit should synchronize. When the convert was admitted into the Christian community by baptism, he turned his back on the pagan life and became a member of a Christian fellowship, founded by Christ. He took the step (as he takes it to-day in the mission field) of his own choice, and at a cost to himself. When we realize what the moment of Paul's own baptism and admission to the Christian Church must have meant to him, as to many another convert, it is no wonder that he mentions the ' sealing ' and the giving of the Spirit as a ' pledge,' as parts of one momentous revolutionary experience.

i. 23–ii. 11 : The Severe Letter and its Result

23 I call God to witness against my soul, it was to spare you that
24   I refrained from revisiting Corinth. (Not that we lord it
ii.   over your faith—no, we co-operate for your joy : you
1   have a standing of your own in the faith.) I decided I
2   would not pay you another painful visit. For if I pain
    you, then who is to give me pleasure ? None but the very
3   people I am paining ! So the very reason I wrote was
    that I might not come only to be pained by those who
    ought to give me joy ; I relied on you all, I felt sure that

my joy would be a joy for every one of you. For I wrote 4 you in sore distress and misery of heart, with many a tear —not to pain you but to convince you of my love, my special love for you. If a certain individual has been 5 causing pain, he has been causing pain not so much to me as to all of you—at any rate (for I am not going to overstate the case) to a section of you. This censure from 6 the majority is severe enough for the individual in question, so that instead of censuring you should now forgive 7 him and comfort him, in case the man is overwhelmed by excessive remorse. So I beg you to reinstate him in 8 your love. For my aim in writing was simply to test you, 9 to see if you were absolutely obedient. If you forgive the 10 man, I forgive him too ; anything I had to forgive him has been forgiven in the presence of Christ for your sakes, in case Satan should take advantage of our position—for 11 I know his manœuvres !

i.

I call God to witness against my soul. The A.V. rendering 23 ' upon my soul ' implies that God knows the real secrets of his heart, and, conscious of such a scrutiny, Paul cannot lie (cf. v. 18). Dr. Moffatt's rendering is also possible, and would mean that, if he is lying, God will punish the perjury. On the whole the former rendering is the more attractive. The 24 apostolic authority which Paul claimed and exercised over the communities he founded, is no soulless official authority. He does not seek to **lord it over your faith.** Religious authority, most of all this apostolic authority, is effective only when the man who exercises it shares allegiance to Christ with those whom he directs, and when his directions are clearly recognized as conveyed to him by Christ Himself. The faith in Christ of the Corinthians themselves enables them to recognize the voice of Christ and the example of Christ in the voice and example of His apostle. **We co-operate for your joy.** Their own faith must co-operate with Paul's faith. Moreover, Paul's anxiety is that they should not only ' believe,' but that they should have **the joy of your faith** (Phil. i. 25). This joy has been absent.

It is necessary to give more than passing attention to Paul's use of the word joy. It has, as in most places in the New Testament, a peculiarly Christian content. Here joy is not synonymous with 'pleasure.' Pleasure is a transient feeling, and ceases with its own gratification. It is pleasure, not joy (as Keats says), 'whose hand is ever at his lips bidding adieu.' 'Wherever there is joy, there is creation : the richer the creation, the deeper the joy. . . . True joy is the feeling of having started an enterprise which goes, of having brought something to life.'[1] It is the joy of the mother who has borne a child, or the merchant who has created a business, or the artist who has painted a picture. Paul thinks of the various Christian communities which came into being as the fruit of his apostolic ministry, as creations of God. 'We are His workmanship, created in Christ Jesus for good works' (Eph. ii. 10). The community at Corinth was one of God's 'new creations'— a fellowship of 'new' men and women. Dominant in Paul's thought of the Church is the thought that God created it. It is not a voluntary association of people who happen to hold the same religious views. Paul's joy is a reflection of the joy of Christ (John xv. 11.; cf. xvi. 20). The apostolic power to bring into being a Christian community had been delegated to Paul by God Himself (cf. 2 Cor. i. 1 ; iii. 56), and any success given to him was accompanied by the joy of creation.

ii.
1   **I decided I would not pay you another painful visit.** The interpretation of these words is so bound up with the interpretation of the whole letter that special and detailed attention must be given to them.

THE PAINFUL VISIT

In 2 Cor. i. 15–ii. 1, Paul devotes some time to explaining why he did not pay a certain visit to Corinth, which was expected. He gives as his reason that he did not wish to pay his Corinthian friends 'another painful visit' (ii. 1). The nature of this painful visit, and the time at which it was

---

[1] H. Bergson, *Mind-Energy*, English translation, p. 23.

made, are questions of much more than academic or chronological interest. The answer we give to them will contribute
largely to the understanding of 2 Corinthians.

(1) Luke records two visits which Paul paid to Corinth.
The first, when the Church was founded, is recorded in Acts
xviii. 1–17. The second visit is recorded in Acts xx. 3, where
Luke says merely that Paul came to Greece, and spent three
months there. Much of this time must have been spent in
Corinth, which he would naturally make his headquarters,
while he visited the Christian communities of ' Achaia '
(2 Cor. i. 1). Neither of these two visits recorded by Luke can
possibly have been the ' painful visit.' Luke's silence, taken
together with other considerations about tô be mentioned,
has led some scholars to assert that the ' painful visit ' never
took place at all. The evidence is based on the grammatical
interpretation of 2 Cor. ii. 1, and other passages.

(*a*) The original of Dr. Moffatt's translation—**I decided I
would not pay you another painful visit**—rendered literally,
reads, ' I decided not again in sorrow to come to you,'
which brings out a possible ambiguity. Grammatically, the
sentence might mean that Paul knew that the particular visit
he now refuses to make would be unpleasant. In that case,
' again ' would be taken with ' come ' instead of with ' in
sorrow.' The former visit would then be Paul's first visit,
when the Church was founded, and Paul shrinks from making
another painful visit (Acts xviii. 6–13).

(*b*) Unfortunately, grammatical ambiguity may also be
detected in two other references Paul makes in this letter to
Corinthian visits—xii. 14 and xiii. 2. Dr. Moffatt translates
the first passage : **Here am I all ready to pay you my third
visit ;** and the second : **This will be my third visit to you.**
So rendered, both passages can only mean that Paul had
actually paid two visits, the latter of which was the ' painful '
one, and was preparing for a third. It is contended, however,
that again it is possible to translate both passages in the sense
that he has been making preparations to come three times,
and has desisted. The first would mean, ' Here am I ready
for the third time to pay you a visit ' ; the second, ' This is the

63

third time I am going to come.' The context, therefore, must be made to settle the matter.

The general context, however, in both cases, seriously impedes the latter interpretation. Both in i. 15 ff., and implicitly in the other two passages, Paul is defending himself against a charge that he has shown an insufficient interest in the affairs of the Corinthian Church. His refusal to pay the visit mentioned in ii. 1, and his going to Macedonia first, is regarded as indicating that he has a greater interest in the Macedonian Churches than in Corinth. In the face of such a charge, it would be intelligible if Paul defended himself by saying that a previous visit was too painful to be repeated. But he is surely too experienced an apologist to bring forward such a weak defence as that he had three times made up his mind to come, had changed it twice, and now threatened actually to arrive.

The difficulty raised by a denial of the ' painful visit ' is also intensified by the immediate context of xiii. 1. The words, on my second visit, in Dr. Moffatt's translation of xiii. 2, are an attempt, fully justified, to remove the vagueness of the A.V. It is true that the Greek is somewhat obscure, and that even in xiii. 2 another rendering is just grammatically possible ; 'I have forewarned, and do now forewarn, as though I were present the second time, although I am now absent.' The last clause, however, in its setting, is a really grotesque statement, besides being otiose. Who would say that he is not present, and then add that he is absent ? Moreover, Paul is not quite so artless a controversialist as to emphasize, under the present circumstances, that he speaks thus strongly *in absentia*. Has he forgotten the charge made against him in x. 9 ? Also, are not the three witnesses of xiii. 1 really a whimsical allusion to three visits ? (see exegetical notes).

(c) It is also contended that the ' painful visit ' never took place, because of Luke's silence regarding it. This is not really a serious objection. If the encounter that took place was of a personal and painful nature, and there were elements in the situation which made it difficult, without much explanation, to set Paul's conduct in retiring from Corinth in an entirely favourable light, it would be quite in accordance with Luke's plan as an historian to omit the incident altogether; especially as the breach was ultimately healed. Luke's aim in Acts is to give only those details of Paul's missionary journeys which would illustrate the general triumphant progress of the Christian mission throughout the Roman world. He does not even enter fully into details of much larger but outgrown controversies, like the controversy regarding the admission of Gentiles. He also gives little indication that Paul endured such a long series of hazards and sufferings as are described in 2 Cor. xi. 23 ff. If he did know any details about the Corinthian affair, he would regard it as a purely domestic matter which deserved no record.

(2) Can we decide when this second, 'painful' visit, took place ?

(*a*) Was it before 1 Corinthians, and indeed prior to the lost letter referred to in 1 Cor. v. 9, as some eminent scholars have supposed ? The lost letter, however, hardly enters into the argument. We know nothing of its contents, save Paul's solitary reference in the first Epistle, and the conjectural fragment of 2 Cor. vi. 14–vii. 1.[1] We have no means of knowing whether it contained any reference to such a visit. We must confine ourselves to the question whether there is any indication of a second visit, already paid, in 1 Corinthians. There is no mention of it. What Paul knows recently of the Church seems to have come to him through members of 'Chloe's household' (i. 11), and through the letter sent him by the Church itself (vii. 1), not by personal knowledge. The only visit of which he speaks in 1 Corinthians is his first one (ii. 1 ; iii. 2 ; xi. 2). Undoubtedly trouble was brewing in the Church (iv. 8 ff.), and Paul's supremacy as leader was threatened (1 Cor. i. 12) ; but there is no indication that he had already had an unpleasant personal experience. Indeed he speaks in iv. 18 as though the encounter with certain 'puffed up' individuals were still to come, and as though he feared that his next visit to Corinth might be an unpleasant one (iv. 21).

(*b*) The visit was not part of any general plan, but incidental, occasioned by some special emergency that had arisen.

---

[1] Cf. p. xv.

There are strong reasons for believing that the ' painful visit ' was unpremeditated. Paul, in 1 Cor. xvi. 5 ff., has previously rejected the idea of a passing visit. There he tells his readers that his present intention is to visit them at the end of a missionary tour in Macedonia, and to remain for some time. Possibly he may even spend the winter in Corinth. He adds that he does not wish to visit them sooner, as he once proposed to do. Such a visit could only be merely in the by-going. The Corinthians were aware of his original intention, and Paul is trying to reconcile their minds to a change of plan. For the sake of clearness, the two plans may be outlined thus :

(A) *The original plan.* He intended to proceed from Ephesus to Corinth, stay a short time there, thence proceed to Macedonia, afterwards returning to Corinth for a longer visit. Thence he would sail to Judea (2 Cor. i. 15 f.).

(B) *The new plan,* announced in 1 Cor. xvi. 5, would eliminate the passing visit to Corinth. He has made up his mind to proceed first to Macedonia, and, after his tour there, arrive at Corinth for a longer visit. The original plan must have been communicated to the Corinthians, either in the first letter, which has been lost (1 Cor. v. 9), or verbally by messenger.

Paul had some good reason for avoiding a flying visit to Corinth. It was no doubt represented to him that, if his authority was to be maintained, he must devote more time and attention to Corinth. It was as though a member of Parliament were accused of neglecting his constituency. The semi-pagan, childish Corinthian temperament would not be likely to share Paul's vision of a world-wide mission. They would readily become jealous of the attention he gave to other places, particularly to Macedonia. A merely passing visit to them in this mood would therefore be worse than useless, and might lead to further misunderstanding. At a later stage, even when the main trouble was over, Paul is accused of 'fickleness' (*elaphria*, 2 Cor. i. 17) in his dealings with Corinth. The word means, not merely change of plan for no particular reason save sudden inclination, but a change which suggests to jealous minds that their interests occupied a secondary place in Paul's heart. His real reason, therefore, for refusing to make the visit expected in i. 15 ff. is that he will not pay another visit, which, because it was so short, might hurt the Corinthians, and serve to revive smouldering embers after the recent conflagration. Clearly Paul has had reason to dread flying visits to Corinth! The 'painful visit' was a real occurrence.[1]

It is also possible that beneath these considerations, there may have lain in Paul's mind an additional reason of a more practical kind. He may have feared that the sea-route from Corinth to Judea, his ultimate destination (1 Cor. xvi. 3 ff.), would be impracticable by the end of October or the beginning of November.[2] By departing from the intention to visit Corinth **merely in the by-going** (1 Cor. xvi. 7)—a plan which the Corinthians still expected him to carry out notwithstanding all that had happened, and perhaps on account of it— he would have longer time, both for the Macedonian tour and ultimately for Corinth, before the winter storms closed the sea-route from Corinth to Judea. Even by adopting the new plan, he saw that it was possible that he might not be able to voyage to Judea that year, and might be compelled to winter in Corinth. Paul may also have been unable to leave Ephesus so soon as he had at first thought, owing to development of his work there, and difficulties which had to be overcome (1 Cor. xvi. 8 f.).

At all events, Paul's previous rejection of the idea of a brief visit to Corinth shows that only a situation of extreme urgency could have induced him to change his mind. The 'painful visit' was not in his original plan.

(3) Was the 'painful visit' an interruption in the course of the journey by way of Macedonia, described by Luke in Acts xix.? (This is clearly the same journey outlined in 1 Cor. xvi.). Or did it take place before the start? What is specially significant for our purpose is that Luke mentions that the journey was deliberately entered upon by the guidance

[1] Cf. G. S. Duncan, *St. Paul's Ephesian Ministry*, pp. 168–175, where there will be found a valuable discussion of the whole situation.

[2] Whatever year is assigned as the date of 1 Corinthians, it was certainly written from Ephesus before Pentecost, i.e. the end of March or the beginning of April.

of the ' Spirit ' (Acts xix. 21), and therefore not lightly to be interrupted. How are we to relate the visit to Corinth, which ended so disastrously, to the plan of this ' inspired ' journey ?

The circumstances seem to have been these. News is suddenly brought to Paul, probably by Timothy (1 Cor. xvi. 10 ff.), at some place unrecorded, that the position at Corinth, which was already giving cause for anxiety, had become very serious. His previous anxiety had induced him to send Timothy ahead of the letter (i.e. 1 Corinthians), not without some misgivings regarding his reception. Whether Timothy handled the situation adequately or not, it is remarkable that Titus, not Timothy, is the next deputy, and carries the ' painful letter.' At all events, the crisis, as Timothy described it—perhaps with ' tears ' (2 Tim. i. 4), which, in contrast with Paul's (2 Cor. ii. 4), were but ' moist impediments to his speech'—had become so grave that Paul felt he must deal with it himself.

Paul must have started on this unexpected visit from the place where Timothy brought him the bad news. Where shall we locate it ? On every ground, the most likely place is Ephesus, which is the traditional opinion.[1] On this view, the journey to Macedonia had not yet been begun when the news reached Paul. This journey may have had to be postponed for at most three weeks. Paul would go straight to Corinth from Ephesus, and return there. At Ephesus also, the severe letter was written. It was sent by Titus, who was asked to meet Paul, already on his way to Macedonia, at Troas with news of its reception and the effect it had produced. By what route Paul journeyed to Troas is not stated, but the time occupied he expected to be long enough for Titus to meet him there on his arrival.[2] At Troas, Paul was greatly disappointed by the non-arrival of Titus. Although the work at Troas was full of promise, he could not go on with it, so great was his anxiety, and instead proceeded to Macedonia (no doubt to Neapolis, the port of Philippi),

---

[1] But cf. G. S. Duncan, *St. Paul's Ephesian Ministry*, pp. 179 ff.

[2] In all probability Paul visited the Churches of the Lycus valley on his way, and during this journey the ' distress in Asia,' to which he refers in 2 Cor. i. 8 ff., may have been encountered.

hoping to meet Titus on his way (ii. 12 f.). Even there he had to wait (vii. 5). At last Titus arrived, the burden was lifted from his spirit, and 2 Cor. i.–ix. was written and despatched.

(4) What happened on the occasion of the ' painful visit ' ? We have seen that the Judaizing emissaries had kindled already inflammable material, and that they probably did not realize that, after undermining Paul's leadership and authority, they would be unable to take his place.[1] Paul, when he arrived, found a condition of chaos and anarchy. Timothy, his delegate who preceded him him, had, we may conjecture, already been badly treated. Paul arrived in order personally to take hold of the situation. He found that there was a seriously organized opposition to his leadership.

The opposition was led evidently by one particular individual (ii. 5 ff.), who seems also to have inflicted on Paul some humiliating personal injury. That he is not to be identified with the incestuous person of 1 Corinthians is certain (see notes on ii. 5 ff.). What really happened is quite obscure, but there can be no doubt that Paul left quickly, and somewhat ignominiously, in circumstances which caused him ' sore distress and misery of heart ' (ii. 4). He had, to quote his words elsewhere, been made ' a fool for Christ's sake,' and neither for the first or last time, **a spectacle to the world, to angels, and to men** (1 Cor. iv. 9). It is, however, quite unwarranted to suggest that his departure was merely a flight. Paul knows, to cite Jerome's words again, 'how to retreat in order to win a victory, to simulate flight in order to slay.'[2] He recognized that he could do no more in person until he had rallied the better elements in the Church on the side of righteousness, and roused the corporate conscience. He commanded the community to discipline the ring-leader themselves, in order to put to the proof their moral sense, and to re-establish their confidence in himself (xiii. 5 ff.). If he had made even a slight impression in this direction before he left, he sought to strengthen and enlarge it by the trenchant exposure of his opponents contained in the same letter. So

[1] p. 27.   [2] p. xxxiv.

effective was this letter, that a stern punishment was inflicted on the principal offender. So excellent was the disciplinary effect on the man himself, that he realized his wrongdoing. A strong reaction set in, in favour of Paul himself. Their loyalty was complete. Paul twice speaks of the 'perfect obedience' of the Corinthians (ii. 9 ; vii. 15). Paul, however, has to intervene, and to plead for mitigation of the man's treatment. He saw that the zeal to show a restored loyalty to himself was leading to undue severity (ii. 11).

2-4   The sore distress and misery of heart, with many a tear, of which Paul speaks, took possession of him as he became conscious that, by the happenings at Corinth, serious hurt was being done to a community which Paul, the apostle of Christ, had founded. The joy that has returned with the healing of the quarrel is 'joy in the Lord.' Once again Christ has triumphed in His servant Paul (cf. ii. 14).

5   The certain individual, who has been causing pain (ii. 5) in the trouble that had arisen, it is well-nigh impossible to identify. That he is not the incestuous person referred to in 1 Cor. v. 1 is certain.[1] It has been conjectured that he was a Church member who had brought a lawsuit before the Roman law-court, instead of laying his case before the local Christian community, for its decision. Recourse to pagan tribunals is forbidden in 1 Cor. vi. 1. There is no direct evidence to support this conjecture, and very little more in favour of the hypothesis that the individual in question is the leader of the Christ party mentioned in 1 Cor. i. 12, a hypothesis supported by a reference to x. 7. If we fail to identify the certain individual, it is at least evident that he had been the ring-leader among those who had flouted Paul's authority, and that he was a member of the local Church. It is also clear that there had been some kind of personal encounter between him

6 and Paul on the occasion of the 'painful visit.' In these verses, Paul shows anxiety to lift the matter out of the region of a personal dispute, and to present it as a matter affecting the whole community (cf. vii. 12). Dr. Moffatt's translation

---

[1] See note on verse 11, and p. xix.

of verse 5 implies that only a majority of the community approved of the severity of the sentence upon the offender whereby he was finally excommunicated. If this translation be adopted, Paul so far agrees with the minority as to ask for mitigation. It is possible, however, to translate verse 5 thus, ' it is not to me alone that he has caused it, but in greater measure or less—I do not wish to overstate the case—he has caused it to you all.' The word translated **majority** might be rendered ' the bulk of his fellows.'[1] This rendering avoids the idea that the community was seriously divided on the moral issue. The contrast is not between a majority and a minority, but between the community and the individual in question. Paul does not say that the punishment was too severe, but that it had lasted long enough. He now bids them reinstate the offender.

The Christian spirit of forgiveness demands much more than 8 correctness of behaviour towards an offender. **Reinstate him in your love,** says Paul. He recognizes that Christ, in the matter of personal injuries, claims control of our inmost feelings, as well as of outward behaviour. Christian forgiveness does not exhaust itself merely in a determined benevolence of bearing towards an offender. Paul is now satisfied that 9 the Corinthians have been **absolutely obedient** to his apostolic authority in thus dealing with the offender, and is anxious lest their renewed loyalty to himself should be accompanied by an excess of zeal, spiritually and morally detrimental to the man himself. **If you forgive the man, I forgive him too.** 10 The words make it plain that some personal insult had been inflicted on Paul during the ' painful visit.' Paul does not mean that his forgiveness is conditional on theirs, but that he also **in the presence of Christ,** and in obedience to His spirit, has forgiven the wrong. He reminds his readers of the same Christian duty that is incumbent on himself. Paul's supreme care now is for the humiliated and penitent offender, for the good name of the Church, and for the honour of Christ. **In 11 case Satan should take advantage of our position**—for I

---

[1] So translated by W. G. Rutherford. The rendering suggested above is also based on Rutherford's translation. Cf. p. xviii.

71

know his manœuvres ! Paul actually thinks of a personal evil power—Satan waiting his opportunity to rob Christ's people of the fruits of Christ's victory. The idea is the same as that which underlies the story of the temptation of Jesus in the Gospels. The Messiah must first meet Satan, who is ready, subtly manœuvring, to appeal to our Lord's own longing for supremacy in the lives of men, and to suggest short cuts to that end. Efforts to remove evil may lead to the ultimate triumph of evil. The powerful discipline which the community has already exercised upon the offender may result in his being overwhelmed with excessive remorse.

The language of verses 10, 11 makes it quite clear that the offender is not the incestuous person of 1 Cor. v. 1 ff. His offence was an injury done to the Christian society. Paul could not have spoken of such an offence as a personal injury which needed personal forgiveness.

ii. 12–17 : Christ's Triumphant Captive

12 Well, when I reached Troas to preach the gospel of Christ,
    though I had a wide opportunity in the Lord, my spirit
13   could not rest, because I did not find Titus my brother
    there ; so I said good-bye and went off to Macedonia.
14   Wherever I go, thank God, He makes my life a constant
    pageant of triumph in Christ, diffusing the perfume of
15   His knowledge everywhere by me. I live for God as the
    fragrance of Christ breathed alike on those who are being
16   saved and on those who are perishing, to the one a deadly
    fragrance that makes for death, to the other a vital frag-
    rance that makes for life. And who is qualified for this
17   career ? I am, for I am not like most, adulterating the
    word of God ; like a man of sincerity, like a man of God,
    I speak the word in Christ, before the very presence of God.

12   Here Paul returns to the narrative begun in i. 8 ff., inter-
    rupted, and begun again in i. 15. At Troas, Titus did not meet
    him, as he expected, with news of the effect of the severe
    letter. Apparently he waited there long enough to begin a new

mission. I had a wide opportunity in the Lord. He was unable to continue. **My spirit could not rest.** Here we have an illuminating glimpse of the heart of Paul. He frankly tells us that he could not settle down to the promising work before him, so long as he was tortured by anxiety regarding his rebellious flock at Corinth. **I said good-bye and went off to 13 Macedonia** in order to meet Titus all the sooner, probably at Philippi. Should he have remained on the spot ? Or did he recognize that the pastor's duty is not merely to make converts, but to secure those he had already made ? Very characteristically, he does not tell us of his meeting with Titus until a few chapters further on (vii. 6 f.). He is dictating 14 the letter, and is suddenly overcome by the remembrance that, whether he was right or wrong to abandon for the moment the work at Troas, God gave him a notable victory at Corinth. Dictation, more readily than writing, allows for sudden changes of thought. He bursts into a paean of praise. **Wherever I go, thank God, He makes my life a constant pageant of triumph in Christ.** Makes my life . . . triumph is the translation of a single word—*thriambeuō*—whose meaning is disputed. The A.V. renders ' causeth us to triumph,' the R.V. ' leadeth us in triumph.' Dr. Moffatt's translation skilfully combines both renderings. Commentators have suggested that Paul has in mind the triumphal welcome given to the victorious Roman general after a victory. The captives were led in chains behind his chariot. If Paul had this Roman triumph in mind, we are met with the logical difficulty that a captive in such circumstances is only a spectacle of humiliation and defeat. It seems better to regard the word as used here in a general sense. Paul uses the same word of Christ's triumph over the ' principalities and powers ' in Col. ii. 15. At the same time, the idea of defeat is not absent from Paul's mind. He loves to combine the idea of defeat and victory in his thoughts about God's dealings with him. ' When I am weak, then am I strong.' God gave this victory at Corinth to a man who had good reason to fear complete defeat. As at other times, it was in weakness that the power of God was fully experienced (cf. 2 Cor. xii. 9).

Hc

73

Paul says that this victorious life is a **pageant of triumph in Christ.** A **triumph in Christ** means just the ' triumph of a Christian man.' To be ' in Christ ' is to be a Christian. Yet Paul's ' in Christ ' is a phrase within which there gleams and burns a stronger flame than our word ' Christian' generally displays. The Pauline ' in Christ ' is very appropriate in connexion with the word ' triumph.' To be ' in Christ,' for Paul, is to share in the powers and glories of that Kingdom or ' reign ' of God which broke in upon the world of time with the death and resurrection of Jesus Christ. To be ' in Christ ' is not merely to follow Christ's steps and teaching as these are traced for us in the documents called the Gospels, or even to have an inward sense of His presence with us. **There is a new creation whenever a man comes to be in Christ** (v. 17). To be ' in Christ,' to be ' led in triumph in Christ,' is no mere mystical union with a risen Christ, where the man's personality is absorbed in Christ's. It is to continue to be a man weak and frail, erring and ignorant, blind and wandering, yet to know that all the power and all the love of God are available for him, and are overruling his life. To be ' in Christ ' means that God **has qualified us to share the lot of the saints in the Light, rescuing us from the power of the Darkness, and transferring us to the realm of His beloved Son** (Col. i. 13). This fundamentally eschatological sense of Paul's frequent expression must not be overlooked.[1]

15 Commentators who hold that Paul is directly referring to the Roman military triumph are in the habit of citing, in elucidation of this verse, the custom of burning incense before the general's chariot as the procession moved through the streets. It is suggested that the odour wafted to the nostrils of the spectators suggested the words, **the perfume of His knowledge.** The suggestion is attractive, but, unfortunately, this accompaniment of a military triumph is mentioned only once, by Appian, an historian of the first century A.D., which forbids us to conclude that it was usual on every occasion. It is much more probable that the metaphor suddenly changes, and that underlying the expressions **perfume of His knowledge** (i.e.

[1] Cf. pp. 113 f.

knowledge of Him) and **fragrance of Christ** there is a sacrificial idea. We may compare Phil. iv. 18., where Paul speaks of the gift of money he has received as a **fragrant perfume, the sort of sacrifice that God approves and welcomes.** The words translated ' fragrant perfume ' are a direct reminiscence of the Septuagint rendering of the story of Noah's sacrifice (Gen. viii. 21 ; cf. Exod. xxix. 18 ; Ezek. xx. 41). Paul is not necessarily thinking of the Old Testament reference, but his language suggests that the original anthropomorphic connotation has become spiritualized in the religious vocabulary. Paul thinks of his life as a sacrificial offering, freely given (cf. Phil. ii. 17). The thought is in line with the idea of surrender to God in the previous verse. It is the effect of his message and of God's goodness and power manifested in his life, upon men, that Paul has before his mind. God is diffusing **the perfume of His knowledge everywhere by me.**

His knowledge means ' knowledge of God,' God revealing His nature and purpose in the Christian gospel. Paul's life of sacrifice and self-surrender reminds men of Christ's sacrifice (cf. notes on i. 5). To Paul's readers, **knowledge** would have certain technical meaning. The various mystery-cults employed the word *gnosis,* or ' knowledge,' to denote that immediate apprehension of God which is obtained by the initiate, and results in ' salvation.' It is a mystical experience rather than a process of thinking. In Phil. iii. 8–10, Paul speaks of fellowship between Christ and his own soul as ' knowing Christ.' Paul may have had the Hellenistic idea of ' knowledge ' in his mind, but his own conception is not drawn from the mystery-religions. It is Jewish, and derived from the prophetic idea of ' knowing God' in the Old Testament. When the prophets speak of God as making Himself known to His people, and of their knowledge of God, they mean that God is known in His inner being. The most complete description of the intimacy of this knowledge is found in Jer. xxxi. 34. Paul, like every missionary, makes use of the appropriate terms in the religious thought of those whom he evangelizes.

This **knowledge** of God is described as a **perfume, a fragrance of Christ.** The term at once suggests that Paul thinks not only of the effect of his preaching, but also of that unseen, insuppressible, pervasive influence, like the odour of a perfume, which goes forth from the lives of those who have the ' grace ' of Christ—His victory, goodness, and joy, in their hearts and lives. Paul is not merely concerned with the uprooting of evil in the Corinthian Church, but is anxious that his ministry should also result in commending his gospel.

15, 16. **What of the words that follow ? Breathed alike on those who are being saved . . . that makes for life.** There are frequent references in later Jewish literature to the Law as a medicine, which heals the pious, but brings death to the man who uses it wrongly. It is laid down that the Law of God, and every commandment in it, should be kept ' for its own sake,' not for any advantage to be gained by it among men or with God. ' He who occupies himself with the teaching of the Law for its own sake, for him it is a life-giving medicine. But whoso does not occupy himself with the teaching of the Law for its own sake, for him it is a deadly poison.'[1] It is regarded as a sin for a man to use for his own ends ' the instrument with which this world and that to come were created.'[2] It is possible that such ideas of the reverence due to the Law, and of the penalty incurred by impious use of it, were part of Paul's Jewish inheritance, and that he applies the same ideas to the Christian gospel. This application, however, is not to be regarded merely as a peculiarity due to his Jewish training. Whatever the source that suggested the language of verses 15, 16, the idea that men's attitude towards the Christian message and Christ's moral teaching raises momentous issues of life and death has proved itself to be the best-attested fact in the world. Christianity is not essentially a body of doctrines or a recital of certain historical events whose power and significance are dependent upon the results of philosophical or historical investigation. These doctrines and events have to do with an historical person, Jesus Christ, who was conscious that in His own person and work an entirely new order in the world's history had made its appearance. He was realizing in His

---

[1] Cf. Strack-Billerbeck, *Commentary on the New Testament*, III. 498.
[2] Cf. G. Foot Moore, *Judaism*, II. 96 f.

own activity and teaching an age-long purpose—the will of God, or Kingdom of God. He knew what God meant Him to do, and He also knew ' that the only future which mattered for men and women depended upon the completion of His task.'[1] In estimating Paul's words here, describing the rejection or misuse of His gospel as containing within itself the element of judgment, we must also remember the lament of Jesus over Jerusalem (Matt. xxiii. 37), and over Bethsaida and Capernaum (Matt. xi. 21 ff.) ; the parable of the two builders (Matt. vii. 24 ff.). It is trifling with history to assert that Paul's sharp alternatives of **those who are being saved** and **those who are perishing, of a deadly fragrance that makes for death and a vital fragrance that makes for life,** are merely interpretation added by a Christian theologian to the simpler and tenderer gospel of Jesus. Paul was not likely to feel, as he says he does, the burden of a gospel ministry which sets out the finality of the contrast between life and death, if there were the least reason to suspect that he had invented the contrast himself, and superimposed on the simpler teaching of Jesus a veil of Jewish dogmatic. The voice that speaks in verse 16 is not the voice of abstract predestinarian doctrine, but the actual result of simple observation of the two contrasted ways in which men receive the Christian message, and of the effects of acceptance or rejection on human character. Paul is here moving in a region of thought where Jesus had dwelt before him. Jesus also beheld men's hearts closing themselves against the love He offered, and their wills rigidly hardening against the will of God. The words in which He speaks of it always vibrate with redemptive passion—**When the Son of Man does come, will He find faith on earth ?** (Luke xviii. 8) ; **The road that leads to life is both narrow and close, and there are few that find it** (Matt. vii. 14 ; cf. Matt v. 29 f., vii. 24–29).

We are apt to be more deeply stirred to-day by the imagination of the tragedy of nations and whole communities, rather than of individuals led by selfish fear and defiant of Christ's teaching, treading the way of death. ' Not with observation ; not where men are pointing, with " Lo here ! Lo there ! "—

[1] E. C. Hoskyns, *The Riddle of the New Testament*, p. 250.

not with the world arrested, silenced into passive and absorbed expectancy, are the great issues of our life to be seen moving towards decision.'[1] Jesus also sees ' all nations ' gathered before Him, but the fateful issue is not in the national, but in the individual, response of their citizens to Himself, irrespective of race. ' Inasmuch as ye did it.' ' Inasmuch as ye did it not.' Communities and nations are just as good as, and no better than, the people who compose them. The real issues of life and death are still being decided in the hearts of individuals, as they react to the personal appeal of Jesus Christ and to the preaching of His gospel on the lips or in the lives of Christian men. These words of Paul's in verse 16 (cf. iv. 4) are not the words of a mere theologian, but of an evangelist who watches with trembling and intense concern what unbelief can do in the lives of men. No wonder that he adds, **And who is qualified for this career ?**

17   The connexion of thought between the closing words of verse 16, **Who is qualified for this career ?** (rather, ' for this charge '), and verse 17 is not quite obvious. Dr. Moffatt has inserted the words **I am**, in an attempt to provide a connexion. The insertion, however, seems to introduce a note of egotism which is unnecessary. The contrast is not so much between men as between their messages. **I am not like most, adulterating the word of God.** (Instead of **like most**, a less exaggerated meaning would be conveyed by ' like too many,' which is a possible translation.) He is referring to the Judaizing emissaries. The noun corresponding to the verb translated **adulterate** means either a 'hawker' or, especially, 'a tavern-keeper.' The word **adulterate** covers the various devices by which wine-sellers deceived their customers. Lucian, who wrote in the second century, accuses the philosophers of ' selling the sciences, too often, like tavern-keepers, blending, adulterating, and giving bad measure.'[2] (The word he uses is the same as in 2 Cor. iv. 2, **falsify**.) Lucian also pillories some of the wandering Christian preachers of his later day, who, he says, ' made quite an income ' by imposing on the simplicity

---

[1] Paget, *Studies in the Christian Character*, p. 94.
[2] *Hermotimus*, 59.

of Christian communities. ' An adroit, unscrupulous fellow, who has seen the world, has only to get among these simple souls, and his fortune is pretty soon made ; he plays with them.'[1] Paul may not mean to accuse his adversaries of making money out of their calling. He certainly accuses them of mingling private interests and prejudices with the work of preaching. The gain they sought may be other than monetary. They may have loved power over other men's lives ; loved to convert them to their particular views. They may have sought admiration for their own intellectual powers. All these motives may be subconscious, and therefore all the more potent. At all events, the attitude is not that of men who are willing that others should cease to listen to them, if they will hear Christ speak. **I speak the word in Christ before the presence of God.**

iii. 1-3 : A Letter of Christ

iii.

Am I beginning again to ' commend ' myself ? Do I need, 1 like some people, to be commended by written certificates either to you or from you ? Why, you are my certificate 2 yourselves, written on my heart, recognized and read by all men ; you make it obvious that you are a letter of 3 Christ which I have been employed to inscribe, *written not with ink but with the Spirit of the living God, not on tablets of stone* but *on tablets of the human heart*.

These verses are of the nature of a parenthesis. The thought 1-3 of ii. 17 is resumed in iii. 4. Paul has evidently been accused of ' commending himself ' whenever he adopts the tone of ii. 14-17.

Written certificates or ' epistles of commendation ' are letters of introduction ordinarily given to those who travelled, either privately or on business, among strangers. The various Christian communities gave such letters to their members as evidence that they were honest people. Apollos carries such letters (Acts xviii. 27), and Paul similarly ' commends '

[1] *Peregrinus*, 13 (Fowler's translation).

Phoebe (Rom. xvi. 1). Paul's opponents evidently brought some introductions of this kind, certainly from the Jerusalem Church, and probably also from other Churches they had visited.

In the thought of these verses two conceptions are mingled : (1) The Corinthian community is Paul's letter of commendation, written on my heart ; (2) The Corinthians are his letters of commendation to the world—a letter of Christ which I have been employed to inscribe (cf. 1 Cor. ix. 1). Not *on tablets of stone* but *on tablets of the human heart* ; a reminiscence of Exod. xxxi. 18, xxxii. 16, xxxiv. 1, and of the New Covenant, Jer. xxxi. 33. It is characteristic of Paul's thinking that the idea of the ' letter of commendation ' suddenly disappears, and the spiritual nature of his ministry, as against the legal ministry of the Old Testament exemplified in the preaching of his opponents, dominates his thought in the rest of the chapter.

iii. 4–11 : A Minister of the New Testament

4 Such is the confidence I possess through Christ in my service
5 of God. It is not that I am personally qualified to form any judgment by myself ; my qualifications come from
6 God, and He has further qualified me to be the minister of a new covenant—a covenant not of written law but of spirit ; for the written law kills, but the Spirit makes
7 alive. Now if the administration of death, which was engraved in letters of stone, was invested with glory—so much so, that the children of Israel could not gaze at the face of *Moses* on account of *the dazzling glory* that was
8 fading from *his face* ; surely the administration of the Spirit must be invested with still greater glory. If there
9 was glory in the administration that condemned, then the administration that acquits abounds far more in glory
10 (indeed, in view of the transcendent glory, *what was*
11 *glorious has thus* no *glory* at all) ; if what faded had its glory, then what lasts will be invested with far greater glory.

The whole argument of these verses is a reflective statement, 4-11 cast in rabbinical form, of the central point at issue between Paul and his opponents. As thus stated, the issue in question shows that the opponents were of the same type as the Judaizers in Galatia. **The written law kills, but the Spirit** 6 **makes alive.** The A.V. rendering, 'the letter killeth, but the Spirit giveth life,' has tended to conceal Paul's actual meaning. There is no reference at all, in Paul's words, to the danger of what is sometimes called the ' literal ' interpretation of Scripture, which makes it unnecessary for the reader to think with his own mind and decide moral questions by the light of his own conscience. As against this attitude, the words are often quoted as meaning that he must, if there is to be life and progress, regard the spirit and purpose of the writer conveyed by his words. All this is quite true, but it is not Paul's meaning. Paul himself sometimes transgresses this excellent principle, when he appeals in rabbinic fashion to the written word of the Old Testament in support of his teaching (e.g. Gal. iii. 13).

In this contrast between the **written law** and **the Spirit,** Paul is contrasting two different kinds of religious authority. He refers to the sense of condemnation, **death,** which a legal religion brings, as contrasted with the spirit of the gospel (cf. Rom. vii. 9-12). The **written law kills** : (1) by imposing an external authority on the inner life ; it merely stimulates sinful impulses ; (2) by holding out no hope of restoration, whereby moral failure may be turned into victory. It imposes punishments for disobedience ; but it gives no power or encouragement to obey. The religion of the Law, says Paul, brought it about that **sin beguiled me and used the command to kill me** (Rom. vii. 11): in other words, to plunge me into moral despair and separate me further from God. The opposing teachers at Corinth were introducing a new legalism into the Christian Church, and probably basing their authority upon their having known Jesus when He lived in the world, and His attitude to the Law, or upon having derived their qualifications from those who had so known Him. The whole subject of **written law** and **spirit** is fully developed in the Epistles to the Romans and Galatians.

THE NEW COVENANT

Covenant, as a term in the vocabulary of our religion, is somewhat unfamiliar to our ears to-day. At first sight, it may seem strange that our translation follows the R.V. in preferring **covenant** to the 'testament' of the A.V. 'Testament' means a will, and to some of Paul's Gentile readers this would be the idea suggested by the Greek word for a will (*diathēkē*), which he uses. Jewish Christians would be likely to understand, as the Greek word just quoted is used in the Septuagint version of the Old Testament to translate the Hebrew word *berith*, or covenant, which has a certain technical meaning. Paul uses the word in this sense, and it is better not to complicate the thought by introducing the idea of a ' will ' or ' testament.'

A ' covenant ' occasionally in Hebrew thought (Hos. ii. 18 ; Gen. xxi. 27), and always in our ordinary language, signifies an agreement between two parties, where each shares the responsibility for its terms. In the Old Testament, however, the word has also prevailingly a technical religious meaning. God makes a covenant with His chosen people, but its terms are determined by God alone. The nation in love and loyalty accepts it. Its inception is an act of God's free favour, and it is inseparably connected with His choice of Israel, out of all the nations of the earth. The covenant is made with the nation regarded as a moral personality, not with the individual. It is embodied in certain legal forms, and involves certain legal requirements. The simplest of these is the Ten Commandments (Deut. v. 2). It also includes the developed regulations for worship which made up Jewish ritual, detailed in Exodus and Leviticus. It goes even deeper, and actually embraces the whole religious and social constitution under which the nation lived—an **administration** (iii. 7.). The covenant in later Hebrew thought represents the point of view of one looking back on ' all the way which the Lord thy God hath led thee ' (Deut. viii. 2, R.V.). The Tabernacle, the Temple and its services, the Law, are Divine institutions, and are the fulfilment in detail of the requirements that are demanded by God's covenant to be the God of Israel. The covenant is His gift. The word might be translated ' religion,' if we may accept the derivation of the word from *religare* = bind. It is a special aspect of religion, as a bond or obligation to serve the god. To the Hebrew, his religion is not a matter of free choice, but was fashioned and given by the free and wonderful favour of Jehovah. This conception is symbolized in the statement that the Ten Commandments were written on the tables of stone by the hand of God Himself (Exod. xxiv. 12 ; Deut. iv. 13) ; or that the pattern of the Tabernacle and its furnishings were shown beforehand to Moses ' in the Mount ' (Exod. xxv. 40), and he must adhere to it rigidly. The written Law, and even in later times, the oral interpretation of it (cf. Matt. xxiii. 2), were God's conception, not man's. Paul himself says that the Law is holy (Rom. vii. 12), i.e. of God's own ordering and the expression of His will.

The permanent and impressive element in the covenant conception is that it is an immutable act of God, who waits to be gracious and changes not. It embodies the Jewish certainty about God, and prepared the way for the Christian certainty or ' new covenant.' This covenant idea lies behind the words, ' This is the true God, and eternal life. My little children, keep yourselves from idols ' (1 John v. 20 f.). Our modern difficulty regarding the conception is due to the fact that so much of our religion is regarded as a quest in the dark, a venture of faith. God is regarded as waiting to be discovered. The Jewish and the Christian conception is that God chooses His people, and reveals Himself to them (cf. John xv. 15 f.). The existence and activity of such a God, the noblest Jewish piety never doubted.

In chapter iii., Paul has particularly in mind the legal aspect of the old covenant-religion. This is, of course, a restricted view. There is, as we have seen, much more than legalism in the religion of the Old Testament. The spiritual experience recorded in psalms and prophecies is of priceless value to the Christian heart. Moreover, we owe to Judaism the deepest of all debts for the conviction embodied in the covenant idea, that religion is revelation, and begins with an act of God, a spontaneous movement of the heart of God towards man ; also for the conviction that religion and morality are insepar- able. Alike in delivering His people from Egypt, and in giving them the Law to obey, we see an exercise of the Divine initiative and sovereignty in redemptive action. Paul else- where amply recognizes this spiritual aspect of Judaism. To the Jew were entrusted the 'promises' of God, fulfilled in Jesus (i. 20). The redemptive activity of God proclaimed in the gospel is attested by the Law and the prophets (Rom. iii. 21). Even the Law is spiritual (cf. vii. 14). ' His profound mind would have thrilled to hear that great word of Jesus, " I am not come to destroy, but to fulfil " ' (Denney).

In considering Paul's sharp and absolute antithesis between the old religion and the new, we must keep two considerations in mind: (1) This contrast of 'letter' and 'spirit' was much more natural in Paul's day than in ours. Christianity now possesses a written law of its own, the ' New Testament of Our Lord and Saviour Jesus Christ,' a collection of documents for the use of the Church. In Paul's day, the gospel was not exposed to the dangers that beset ' book ' religion.[1] It was a spoken word living on the lips and in the lives and hearts of men. At the most, there could have been in existence only a few short written collections of sayings of Jesus, and of stories of His life.

(2) Another important consideration is that Paul is speaking out of his former experience as a Pharisee. To the Pharisee of Paul's day, the Old Testament scriptures had acquired the character of a statutory document. The Law was written in letters on sheets of parchment, and Paul had been instructed from his youth to take its imperatives seriously. In these pre- Christian days, he never seems fully to have penetrated the secret of Jeremiah's haunting and torturing sense of the failure of the old statutory religion, or to have shared his vision of a new spiritual religion. ' I will put My law in their inward parts, and in their heart will I write it : and I will be their

---

[1] Cf. the essay in *Aspects of the Greek Genius* (S. H. Butcher) on ' The Written and the Spoken Word,' where the theme of the Greek depre- ciation of the written word is developed.

God, and they shall be My people' (Jer. xxxi. 31 f.). It is probable that Paul took the expression **new covenant**, not from Jeremiah, but from Our Lord's words at the Last Supper. **God has qualified me to be the minister of a new covenant.** Both Luke (xxii. 20) and Paul (1 Cor. xi. 25) agree in quoting the words. 'This cup is the new covenant in My blood.' Paul rarely uses the word 'covenant' elsewhere in his letters, but he introduces us here to the dominant and inspiring idea in his whole conception of Christianity as centred in the death and resurrection of Christ. A 'new covenant' is a new religion. It stands for the breaking in upon the world of a new spiritual order. God's relationship to man is based on a new constitution. God made a new covenant with men when, in Christ, He offered free forgiveness of sin, made fellowship with Himself accessible to all, and opened up the secret of obedience as an instinctive response to the self-revelation of God in Christ.

The key-word in this passage is **glory.** **The administration** 7-11 (or 'dispensation') **of the spirit** possesses a **glory** superior to the glory of the old covenant. It is the glory of a final and eternal religion as distinct from a glory which belongs to a religion which is imperfect and temporary (cf. verse 15). **Glory** is a plastic word, whose meaning often eludes us, unless we realize that it alternates between the sense of a visible outward manifestation of God and a manifestation of His character and purpose, spiritually apprehended. The 'glory of God' means essentially the life or energy of the living God self-revealed (cf. Rom. vi. 4). The 'glory' of the new religion is determined by the medium through which it is manifested—**the knowledge of God's glory in the face** [or personality] **of Christ** (iv. 6). Both the glory on the face of Moses and the glory of **the administration of the Spirit** are symbols of a self-revelation of God. The glory of God in the Old Testament is not a purely self-centring conception. God is said to be glorified 'not when his goodness is revealed to men, and they admire or praise it ; for that would still involve a certain egoism. He is glorified when by revealing His goodness He attracts men unto Himself, and His own goodness is reproduced in them, and they are created anew in His image.'[1] The ' grace ' of God, and its success in subduing men to His gracious purpose, is **to the praise of His glory** (Eph. i. 12, 14). The *dazzling glory* in the Old Testament story (Exod. xxxiv. 29–35) is an external physical manifestation of the Divine on the face of Moses. It is interpreted by Paul as a symbol of the moral glory of the old covenant which yet failed to make men like itself. On the other hand, the glory of the new covenant is one that actually transforms men from **one glory to another** (verse 18.). It should not escape notice that, in comparing the gospel he preached with the religion of the Old Testament, Paul assumes that he himself is a person no less distinguished than Moses (iv. 6) ; a claim that must have appeared to his opponents extraordinarily audacious.

This alternation of meaning between the physical and the spiritual in Paul's conception of ' glory ' is disturbing to our thought. He was not accustomed to make our sharp distinction between the two. ' Glory ' to him is just a ' radiant self-expression ' of the Divine, whether sensible or spiritual. Stephen's face is said to have **shone like the face of an angel,** reflecting the Divine glory. Paul's use of the term is probably affected by an impression which is derived from his conversion-experience, and gives the word in his writings a certain quasi-physical significance.[2]

9 **The administration that acquits** reproduces the technical meaning of ' righteousness ' in the Pauline thought.[3] ' Justify' is the translation of the Greek verb that corresponds to the noun translated ' righteousness.' It is used of a judge who vindicates one who is wronged. In the Pauline sense, ' justify' means to acquit one who is not wronged, but is ' in the wrong ': i.e. the sinner. The ' righteousness of God ' in Paul's religious vocabulary means that God ' puts men in the right '—i.e. with Himself. He ' justifies ' men. In other words, He offers free forgiveness to sinful men. God does not ' make men

---

[1] A. B. Davidson, *The Theology of the Old Testament*, p. 174.
[2] Cf. H. A. A. Kennedy, *St. Paul and the Mystery-Religions*, pp. 192 ff.
[3] Cf. C. H. Dodd, The Moffatt Commentary, *Romans*, pp. 9–13.

righteous,' but restores them to that immediate fellowship with Himself through which righteousness is possible. He acquits men, in terms of this new covenant, so that the sense of guilt and of bondage to past sin no longer disables men morally, nor robs them of the will and power to do His will.

iii. 12–18 : The Unveiled Face

Such being my hope then, I am quite frank and open—not like 12- Moses, who *used to hang a veil over his face* to keep the 13 children of Israel from gazing at the last rays of a fading glory. Besides, their minds were dulled, for to this very day, 14 when the Old Testament is read aloud, the same veil hangs. Veiled from them the fact that the glory fades in Christ ! Yes, down to this day, whenever Moses is read aloud, the 15 veil rests on their heart ; though *whenever they turn to the* 16 *Lord, the veil is removed.* (The Lord means the Spirit, 17 and wherever the Spirit of the Lord is, there is open 18 freedom.) But we all mirror *the glory of the Lord* with face unveiled, and so we are being transformed into the same likeness as Himself, passing from one glory to another— for this comes of the Lord the Spirit.

Not like *Moses* who *used to hang a veil over his face* to keep 13 the children of Israel from gazing at the last rays of a fading glory. Paul here employs a traditional rabbinic method of interpretation, whereby the words of Scripture are interpreted allegorically for the purpose of edification. There is nothing in the Old Testament story of Exod. xxxiv. 33 ff. to suggest that Moses veiled his face with this motive in view. The actual motive in the Exodus narrative is based on a primitive superstitious notion that the veil was used in order that the people might not be injured or die by too long exposure to the dangerous Divine rays (cf. Exod. xxxiv. 30 ; 2 Sam. vi. 6 f.). Paul's interpretation is hardly more religious. He cannot be acquitted of a clever attempt to score off his opponents.[1] The idea is a sudden tangent of thought which would neither

[1] Cf. pp. xxxiii. f.

convince nor conciliate them. He can hardly mean to accuse Moses of subterfuge, but treats him like a lay figure. In verse 7, he allows to stand, alongside his words here, a tribute to the ' glory ' with which even **the administration of death** was invested.

14 Having given this side-thrust, Paul describes the **veil** that
15 hangs for the Jew over the sacred book, and rests also on their hearts, hiding the dawn of the new day in Christ. The
16 glory fades in Christ : *whenever they turn to the Lord, the veil is removed.*[1]

17 **The Lord means the Spirit.** Whom does Paul mean by **the Lord,** here and in the previous verse ? God or Christ ?

(1) It is held that in both passages God is meant. It is to God that Moses went in unveiled. Paul, it is said, allegorizes rather freely the words of Exod. xxxiv. 34, as he quotes them freely. When Israel turns to the Lord, the veil will be removed from their hearts. The self-revealed glory of God is practically equivalent to the Spirit of God, the Spirit of the new covenant which is life-giving. The clause is regarded as explanatory, indicating that **turn to the Lord** means turn in response to the gift of sonship (Rom. viii. 15 ; Gal. iv. 6). Moreover, although 'Lord' is usually the title of Jesus in the Pauline writings, it is used of God in viii. 19 ; Phil. iv. 4 ; 2 Thess. ii. 13, and elsewhere. ' Lord ' is rarely used alone of Jesus, but mostly in conjunction with the personal name, Jesus Christ— ' Our Lord Jesus Christ.'

(2) Another interpretation is that in both verses **the Lord** is Christ. **The Lord means the Spirit** identifies Jesus and the Spirit, at least in the experience of men. **The Lord** is the risen and exalted Jesus, upon whom God has conferred ' the name which is above every name ' (Phil. ii. 9 ff.). Moreover, it may be contended, the Jews did not need to turn to Jahveh, but to Christ. In Rom. viii. 9–11 the life of Christ in the Christian is identified with the life of the Spirit. On the whole, this second view is preferable. If it be adopted, the

---

[1] There is a mistranslation—' till ' for ' when '—in the A.V. of Exod. xxxiv. 33. The sense of the A.V. is the exact opposite of Paul's interpretation.

term Lord in verse 16 hovers between a reference to God and to Christ. In other words, Paul sees in the Old Testament words of Exod. xxxiv. 34 an allegorical reference to Christ. Two things ought to be said : (1) We cannot read developed Trinitarian ideas into Paul's thinking. He has in view not the person of Christ so much as His power. In the O.T., 'Lord' does not denote God's essential being, but His power. In Paul's thought, the Spirit is not a distinct theological entity, but God in redeeming action and movement upon the human heart. In the experience of men, the power of God, of the exalted Christ, and of the Spirit are identical. God has conferred upon Christ His own name, **Lord** (Phil. ii. 11). Therein we have the raw material of subsequent Trinitarian doctrine. Paul is here moving in the region of unanalysed experience. (2) This identification in experience of the risen Christ and the Spirit has an important bearing on Paul's doctrine of the Spirit. By thus identifying the Spirit as the spirit of Jesus, he teaches that speaking in tongues and other miraculous phenomena do not include the whole range of the Spirit's manifestations. The Christian life is regarded as equally miraculous with the speaking in tongues. The 'fruit of the Spirit' are those qualities of character which are found in Jesus Christ (Gal. v. 22 f.). **Wherever the Spirit of the Lord is, there is open freedom.** Christian freedom is not the abolition of all constraint. It is the acceptance of a new constraint, which operates not from without, but from within. It is **open freedom,** not enforced, but free acceptance of the will of God (cf. John viii. 31 ff.). It is the end of legal religion. Intellectual freedom is included. Whatever additional content Christian experience may have, the exercise of private judgment and freedom to select our authorities are indispensable conditions of its vitality. The Christian does not merely accept certainties, but discovers them.

We all mirror *the glory of the Lord* **with face unveiled. 18** There are three contrasts in these words : (1) we as opposed to Jews ; (2) all in contrast with one individual—Moses ; (3) **with face unveiled.** No veil hangs between our eyes and the

' glory ' or self-revelation of God in the person of Christ. The R.V. and the A.V. give different translations of the word translated mirror. ' Reflecting as a mirror,' and ' beholding in a glass.' Dr. Moffatt's translation agrees with the R.V., which seems to be demanded by the context, although both senses of the word are found. The relevant idea is that Christians, unlike Moses, do not require to ' veil their faces ' when the *glory of the Lord* shines upon them. Neither do they need to conceal from others their changed condition. The Christian life is a continual testimony to the world. So we are being transformed into the same likeness as Himself. The glory of God manifested in Christ, is creative. The transformation comes of the Lord the [creative] Spirit. Again, in experience, the Spirit of God and the risen Christ are one redemptive agency (cf. iv. 6). The change takes place through the growth in Christian faith and character, from one glory to another.

As in Rom. viii. 29, Phil. iii. 21, Paul's language may owe something to the idea, prominent in the various mystery-religions, of transformation by the vision of God. Paul must have grown familiar with their terminology, and, as a missionary, would make use of conceptions familiar to his converts. But Paul always re-mints what he borrows. His emphasis here is on the *moral* significance and power of the Divine glory. The emphasis in the mystery-religions is laid upon a quasi-magical transmutation of essential being.[1]

iv. 1–6 : THE CREATIVE DAWN

iv.

1 Hence, as I hold this ministry by God's mercy to me, I never
2   lose heart in it ; I disown those practices which very
    shame conceals from view ; I do not go about it craftily ;
    I do not falsify the word of God ; I state the truth openly
    and so commend myself to every man's conscience before
3   God. Even if my gospel is veiled, it is only veiled in the

[1] Cf. H. A. A. Kennedy, *St. Paul and the Mystery-Religions*, p. 183.

case of the perishing ; there the god of this world has 4
blinded the minds of unbelievers, to prevent them seeing
the light thrown by the gospel of the glory of Christ, who
is the likeness of God. (It is Christ Jesus as Lord, not 5
myself, that I proclaim ; I am simply a servant of yours
for Jesus' sake.) For God who said, ' Light shall shine 6
out of darkness,' has shone within my heart to illuminate
men with the knowledge of God's glory in the face of
Christ.

Paul returns again to the theme with which he started in 1-6
chapter iii.—the apostolic ministry entrusted to him. It is
evident that he had been accused of ' veiling ' (verse 3) the
real content and meaning of his message. His opponents 2
maintained that his doctrine of spiritual freedom led to
immorality, and that he refused to **disown** certain **practices**
which had invaded the Corinthian Church. **Which very
shame conceals from view** may mean either that shame makes
a man conceal them, or, better, that shame prevents his
speaking of them openly. Paul further repels a charge of
' craftiness,' or the use of artifice. **I do not falsify the word of
God.** The reference here may be to charges made against his
use of the Old Testament as supporting the idea of the tran-
sience of the Law (cf. note on iii. 13). **I state the truth
openly . . . before God.** The meaning is that he does not
bring his own interpretations into prominence by unworthy
means, but the truth which he proclaims appeals to **every
man's conscience**—rather, to 'every human conscience.' Some 3
consciences are insensitive, and the ' veil ' which prevents his
gospel reaching the consciences of some is spread by **the god of** 4
this world—i.e. the Evil One. Paul shares the contemporary
belief that the present **world,** or ' age,' has been temporarily
given over by God Himself to the power of the Devil. His
aim is to blind **the minds of unbelievers** so that they may not
recognise **the light of the gospel of the glory of Christ.** Christ's
glory is that, in fulfilment of God's purpose, He came to deliver
men from the power of the Devil. At other times Paul speaks
of a hierarchy of evil powers, **the Powers of this world** (1 Cor. ii.

91

6 ff.). Christ's glory is also God's glory, because He is the likeness of God.[1] The glory of God is His saving power exercised in
Christ. The aim of the evil powers is to rob man of this deliver-
5 ance or 'salvation.' Paul's enemies had evidently been asserting that he presumptuously proclaimed his own phantasies, and
that the vision on the Damascus road was a product of his own
6 imagination. Hence the remarkable words of the following
verse. Paul never refers in his letters to the details of the
conversion-experience recorded in Acts. He concentrates
upon the light from heaven (Acts xxvi. 13) which shone within
my heart (not 'our hearts' as in A.V., cf. p. xxxv.). 'Whatever
occurred, Paul brought it to the test of as sound judgment
and as searching experiment as a whole life of verification
allowed' (T. R. Glover). The sum of that judgment is given
us in this verse. The source of light was the same creative
power that, with the words 'Let there be light,' brought order
out of chaos at the beginning of all things. Paul here speaks
of his own unique qualification to be a minister of Christ. The
creative power in his own new life was God's glory in the face
[or 'person'] of Christ. His mission is to illuminate men, to
bring light out of darkness. Here Paul goes as far as human
words can go, in stating his conviction that the message entrusted to him inaugurates an entirely new creative era in the
world's history. From the lofty height of his apostolic
mission, he can set his own estimate on even the work of
Moses, the most notable figure in Jewish religion.

iv. 7–12 : A Dying Man and a Living Christ

7 But I possess this treasure in a frail vessel of earth, to show that
the transcending power belongs to God, not to myself ;
8 on every side I am harried but not hemmed in, perplexed

---

[1] Paul believed that he had actually seen the heavenly Christ with the
bodily eye (1 Cor. ix. 1). There is a blending of the sensible and the
spiritual in his description of the experience, which is apparent in this
passage. The **body of his Glory** (Phil. iii. 21) is more than metaphor.
This blending of what to our minds seem two different kinds of perception must always be borne in mind in our interpretation of Paul's
thought. Cf. the notes on iv. 16–18.

but not despairing, persecuted but not abandoned, struck 9
down but not destroyed—

wherever I go, I am being killed in the body, as Jesus 10
was,

so that the life of Jesus may come out in my body :

every day of my life I am being given over to death for 11
Jesus' sake,

so that the life of Jesus may come out within my
mortal flesh.

In me then death is active, in you life.   12

Paul has been describing the **glory** of his apostolic minis- 7
try. Swiftly there rises in his mind the contrast between this
treasure and his own personality, **a frail vessel of earth**, in
which it is borne. Paul's enemies had cruelly attacked his
personal appearance (x. 1, 10) and his lack of the graces of
the orator (x. 10 ; xi. 6). The recurrent malady to which he
refers (xii. 7) must often seriously have disabled him. Yet
he must have possessed a certain toughness of physique to
enable him to sustain long trying journeys, and such hardships as he describes in xi. 23 ff.

In an apocryphal collection of apostle-legends, written in
the latter half of the second century, called the *Acts of Paul
and Thekla*, there is a description of Paul's personal appearance. It is said that one called Onesiphorus of Iconium went
out to meet Paul, who was expected in that city. As he
scanned the faces of the passers-by, he sees, " coming along,
a man of moderate stature, with curly (or crisp) hair and
scanty ; crooked legs ; with blue eyes ; and large knit eye-
brows ; long nose ; and he was full of the grace and pity of
the Lord, sometimes having the appearance of a man, but
sometimes looking like an angel.'[1]

It would be a mistake, however, to think that the 'earthenware

---

[1] Translated by T. R. Glover, *Paul of Tarsus*, p. 172 (cf. W. M.
Ramsay, *Church in the Roman Empire*, pp. 33 f.). It is very probable
that this description is based upon a very early tradition ; all the more
likely that there are no less than four texts of it in different languages,
with interesting slight variations, additions, and omissions.

vessel' is a symbol only of physical frailty. Paul tells us of doubts, and fears and tears ; of being crushed more than I could stand (i. 8) ; of the strain of things (vii. 5). There is moral weakness as well. ' The good that I would I do not ; but the evil which I would not, that I do,' is a description of moral struggle applicable, we may be sure, not only to his experience in unregenerate days. It is not only his bodily frailty which sets forth that the transcending power belongs to God. Paul had limitations and confusions

8-9both of mind and will. The description in verses 8, 9 suggests both inward and bodily weakness. In these verses we can see Paul in the hands of a brutal mob, chased through the narrow streets, or stoned and left for dead (Acts xiv. 19). We can also imagine the nerve-strain, the sense of abandonment, and the resentment which such treatment would bring. Yet, for each word describing his own weakness, he finds another which celebrates the ' excellency of the power of God ' that delivered him. This deliberate choice of contrasted words reveals a consciousness that even such painful and sordid experiences belong to a life which is a constant pageant of triumph in Christ (ii. 14).

10 Paul sums up all his experiences of human frailty in remarkable words. Dr. Moffatt's translation, I am being killed in the body as Jesus was, is a free but both necessary and adequate paraphrase of the Greek which is more literally rendered in the A.V.—' always bearing about in the body the dying of Jesus.' Paul thinks of all the strain, shame, and pain that were the lot of Jesus in the closing days. What is in his mind is the profoundly comforting and moving thought that ' the disciple is not above his master ' (Matt. x. 24). Paul says ' dying ' and not ' death.' He thinks of the treatment Jesus received from men. The use of the personal name Jesus is remarkable. It is an indication that he is well acquainted with the Passion story, and that in some intimate moments of his life he found strong consolation in dwelling upon it. His deep pre-occupation with the death and resurrection of Jesus is founded upon an historical basis. The words of Newton's hymn.

94

How sweet the name of Jesus sounds
In a believer's ear !
It soothes his sorrows, heals his wounds,
And drives away his fear,

are charged with much more than sentimental meaning.

That the life of Jesus may come out in my body. Paul still has in mind the contrast between the frail vessel of earth and the transcending power of God. In these verses he reveals the secret source of his own endurance and victory. It is the ' life-energy ' that comes from the living and reigning Jesus ; the same inward power of God that sustained Jesus in his trials on earth, which also makes Paul strong when he is weak. **Every day of my life, I am being given over to death** 11 **for Jesus' sake.** All the excitement of these dangers and escapes, these distresses of soul, these sufferings, are sapping his strength and bringing him nearer the grave. He is **being killed in the body as Jesus was,** but within him, too, there is a Divine resurrection power at work. The best commentary on this passage is found in Paul's own words : **I would know Him in the power of His resurrection and the fellowship of His sufferings, with my nature transformed to die as He died, to see if I too can attain the resurrection from the dead** (Phil. iii. 10 f.). There also hovers around the words, **so that the life of Jesus may come out in my body** . . . **within my mortal flesh** (with all its sinfulness), the thought that, through what the Christian believer is enabled to be and to endure, testimony is borne before men to the reality of his faith. **In me then death is active, in you life,** is by no means 12 ironical (as Calvin thought). It is the preacher's testimony that, not only words, but a sacrificial life is needed to enable his hearers to share in the ' life abundant ' which Jesus came to bring.

iv. 13–18 : Trials are Visible but Transient

But since our spirit of faith is the same, therefore—as it is 13 **written** *I believed and so I spoke*—**I too believe and so I speak, sure that He who raised the Lord Jesus will raise** 14

me too with Jesus and set me at your side in His presence.
15   It is all in your interests, so that the more grace abounds,
the more thanksgiving may rise and redound to the glory
16   of God.   Hence I never lose heart ; though my outward
man decays, my inner man is renewed day after day.
17   The slight trouble of the passing hour * results in a solid
18   glory past all comparison, for those of us whose eyes are
on the unseen, not on the seen ; for the seen is transient,
the unseen eternal.

13   **Our spirit of faith is the same.**   Two interpretations are
possible : (1) Paul has the same faith as the Psalmist whom
he quotes ; (2) He has the same faith as his readers.   The
second interpretation is on the whole more likely.   In the
previous verse, Paul has been contrasting his experience with
that of the Corinthians.   Now he emphasizes what they have
in common.   Their ' life,' ministered to them by the witness
his endurance bears to the power of the living Christ, produces in them the same faith which Paul exercises.   Even if
death overtakes Paul, he and they believe—for so he would
14 have them believe—that God **will raise me too with Jesus
and set me at your side in His presence.   I believed and so
I spoke.**   Paul quotes from the Septuagint version of the
Psalm (cxvi. 10).   The Hebrew version is obscure, but may
mean ' I believed and so I spoke '—i.e. spoke despairingly as
in the words that follow : ' I was greatly afflicted : I said in
my haste, All men are a lie ' (R.V.) (see Dr. Moffatt's translation).   Probably Paul has the whole passage (Ps. cxvi. 10 ff.)
in mind, although his own utterance in verses 10–12 is really
in a different vein from the Psalmist's.   Paul does not always
quote the Old Testament in its exact reference, and often
seems to quote from memory.   The reference to his own
resurrection is to resurrection at the great moment, not far
distant, when the risen Jesus, who is ' at the right hand of
God,' will return in power, and **will bring with Him those
who have fallen asleep** (1 Thess. iv. 14).   Apparently Paul at
the moment believes that he may be among **those who are**

* Omitting $\dot{\eta}\mu\hat{\omega}\nu$.

asleep in death at the Great Day. This resurrection, of an apostle whom his work is killing, crowns the contrast between the frail vessel of earth, Paul's mortal body, and the transcending power of God.

It is all in your interests. Paul seeks to point out that he 15 is not thinking merely of his own personal salvation and vindication. All that happens to him has an echo in their thanksgiving, rising out of his own experience of grace that abounds. This thanksgiving is a testimony to the world, when it is seen to rise and redound to the glory of God. *Though my outward man decays, my inner man is renewed* 16 *day by day.* By the inner and the outward man, Paul simply means that there is a profound distinction to be made between what happens to a man, either in his own body or in outward circumstances, and the inner man, the complete personality who reacts to the outward environment. What Paul really says is that faith in the ultimate and final victory of Jesus over death, and the indestructibility of the Divine purpose for the world, means for the believer participation in that victory. Paul's universe, or, as we might say, his view of nature, is not conceived, like our own, in terms of impersonal natural law, either inherently active, or under the control of a personal Deity. His universe is conceived as an organism of personal existences. Paul speaks of 'angels,' 'principalities,' 'powers.' At times he personifies 'sin' and 'death.' Above their temporary sway, the personality of the risen Jesus reigns supreme, and those who are united to Him in faith and experience—in the inner man—are assured of 'salvation' which includes immortality. The powers of the 'age to come' are already at work in the lives of believers. The life of Jesus already comes out within their mortal flesh. *The* 17 *slight trouble of the passing hour* is contrasted with a *solid glory past all comparison.* We must bear in mind that these are also the terms of the contrast between the seen and the unseen in the following verse. Slight is the same word as in 'my burden is light' (Matt. xi. 30). *The passing hour* renders well the implication in Paul's mind that the time between now and the dawn of the Great

Day is brief. Paul boldly reverses the usual human values.
'We are accustomed to think of affliction as what lasts,
and of the strength to endure as fitful and transient. For
Paul the ' permanence is on the other side ' (Plummer). The
A.V. translates : ' an eternal weight of glory.' The idea of
' weight,' a heavy burden, is certainly in Paul's mind. Does
not he again sharply reverse human values ? We think of
the body, when we are exhausted or sick, as a burden. Paul
thinks of the glory of the life to come, already in some measure
his, as a burden, conceived as we might speak of a ' burden
of song,' of a tree ' burdened ' with fruit, or of the sea, once
a burden to the man who is learning to swim, but actually
sustaining him when he does learn. Wings are not a burden
to the full-grown bird. Paul may also have in his mind the
idea of a scale. ' Weighed against one another, the glory goes
down and the affliction kicks the beam ' (Plummer). It is
also possible that he may be playing upon the Hebrew word
for ' glory ' (*kaboth*), which is cognate with the verb ' to be
heavy.' The two ideas are similarly conjoined in our phrase,
' heavy with splendour.' This verse is an expansion of the
18 same idea. **The seen** is just the sum of the tribulations past
and present of which his life is full. **The unseen** is not just
vaguely everything that is hidden from mortal eyes. For
Paul **the unseen** is just the whole significance of the living
Christ, now reigning and triumphant over all that makes men
afraid. Like the author of Hebrews, Paul would say, **we do
not yet see all things controlled by man ; what we do see is
Jesus** (ii. 9). ' He reigns more for us than for Himself ' (Calvin). Human frailty and suffering are visible, but **transient.
The unseen is eternal.**

There is an unmistakable rhythm in the words of verses
16–18, a rhythm which often makes itself felt when Paul is
deeply moved. The parallelisms are the parallelisms of
Hebrew poetry. The **outward man**, the seen at this particular
moment, is a man who wears all the signs of nervous exhaustion
and physical strain. We would say, as he says of himself,
that he has not long to live. Yet our **eyes** are inevitably
fixed **on the unseen**, because his are so fixed. A strange,

indestructible, spiritual energy appears from some hiding-place within the frail body. ' Through the lines and furrows of his face gleams a spiritual glory of the soul. It flashes out from the deep-set, keen, piercing eyes, making us think at once of Dürer's portrait of the apostle ' (Boussett).

v. 1–10 : The Spirit a Pledge of Immortality

v.

I know that if this earthly tent of mine is taken down, I get a 1 home from God, made by no human hands, eternal in the heavens. It makes me sigh indeed, this yearning to be 2 under the cover of my heavenly habitation, since I am 3 sure that once so covered I shall not be ' naked ' at the hour of death. I do sigh within this tent of mine with 4 heavy anxiety—not that I want to be stripped, no, but to be under the cover of the other, to have my mortal element absorbed by life. I am prepared for this change by God, 5 who has given me the Spirit as its pledge and instalment. Come what may, then, I am confident ; I know that while 6 I reside in the body I am away from the Lord (for I have 7 to lead my life in faith, without seeing Him) : and in this 8 confidence I would fain get away from the body and reside with the Lord. Hence also I am eager to satisfy Him, 9 whether in the body or away from it ; for we have all to 10 appear without disguise before the tribunal of Christ, each to be requited for what he has done with his body, well or ill.

This earthly tent of mine. Paul now proceeds to develop 1 the thought of the **outward** and the **inner man**, by means of the contrast between **this earthly tent** and **a home from God, made by no human hands.** The **yearning** is itself part of 2 Paul's assurance of the reality of the **heavenly habitation.** In the following verse the terms of the contrast begin to 3 alternate with the idea of a robe. The alternation is perplexing to the reader, as is also the fact that Paul appears to be developing his thought at once from two different points of view. One is the view of those who expect to be alive at Christ's Appearing, the other of those who, like himself in his present mood, may be in their graves. Both points of view, however, are for him really one. In both living and dead, at the Appearing, there will be a great and decisive ' change ' (I Cor. xv. 52 f., cf. verse 5). As an alternative to being **under the cover of my heavenly habitation,** Paul speaks of being ' **naked** ' **at the hour of death.** It has been suggested that by **naked** Paul indicates a period of waiting, an intermediate state in which the body of flesh and blood is no more, and the ' body of glory ' is not yet ours ; as when he speaks of **those who are asleep in death** (I Thess. iv. 13). There is, however, no reason to think that Paul ever speculated deeply on this subject. He had no need to do so. For him the time of waiting was brief, and the coming of Christ was near.[1] The utterance here is not speculation, but the momentary expression of a very human fear.

4   Note that it is *personality* in the future life with which Paul is concerned. His mind recoils from the idea of being a disembodied spirit. In the older Hebrew notion of Sheol, the abode of the dead, the spirits are without definite form or organs of expression and activity—paralysed personalities. Dr. Moffatt puts 'naked' in verse 3 in inverted commas, which may be taken to imply a reference to such a condition. **Not that I want to be stripped** may mean that Paul is possessed by the human longing to escape the dreary and repellent experience of dying, the shedding of the body of flesh. If so, his outlook on death is not the rather shallow one of those who ' make quick-coming death a little thing.' Paul is very human when he thus shrinks from the moment of dissolution. Whatever theories of the relation of soul and body may be ascribed to Paul, here he just thinks of the moment of dying in a very real and human way. He does not conceive it as like passing ' from one room to another.' Paul would rather have his **mortal element absorbed by life**—i.e. at the Parousia. Paul's thinking on these subjects often stops short at the point where we would like him to continue. It is possible that the many narrow escapes from death he had had, and the sense of growing

[1] Cf. H. A. A. Kennedy, *St. Paul's Conception of the Last Things,* p. 266.

bodily weakness and exhaustion, had turned his thoughts to the fact that he may have the experience of dying, instead of living to see the Great Day of the Lord's Appearing. What happens after death does not greatly concern him. He says unmistakably that death cannot bring the believer into any region or state where he is separated from Christ. The fellowship may be for the moment imperfect from the point of view of the ' glory which shall be revealed ' (Rom. viii. 18), but the condition is not one to excite fear or apprehension. **Death is to be with Christ** (Phil. i. 23). **We are the Lord's, whether we live or die** (Rom. xiv. 9).

To have my mortal element absorbed by life. These words are quite insufficient to support any theory as to the relation between the mortal and the spiritual body. The spiritual robe is not conceived as a Nessus garment which consumes the material of the body of flesh. He does mean that in the experience of dying, as at the Appearing of Christ (1 Cor. xv. 52), we shall be done with our earthly bodies. Yet, in Paul's view, this body is not, as in the Greek conception, the ' tomb ' or ' prison-house ' of the soul, release from whose grosser material is the condition of spiritual bliss. Paul thinks here of the bodily life generally as an experience of frailty, which will no longer be present in the future life. Whatever is Paul's view as to the physical connexion between the earthly and the spiritual body, there is a moral nexus between them. A man is held responsible for **what he has done with his body** (verse 10 ; see notes).

I am prepared for this change by God. Again Paul gives 5 no material for analysing the nature of his preparation. It is going on even now in the renewal of his **inner man day after day.** It is the work of the Spirit, which God gives **as its pledge and instalment.** ' Pledge ' and ' instalment ' are one word in Greek (' earnest,' A.V., R.V.). The word is a commercial term, meaning a token payment in guarantee that the whole amount is ultimately due. The ' Spirit ' is the animating principle of the ' spiritual,' as distinct from the ' natural,' man (1 Cor. ii. 15). Paul means that his ' spiritual ' personality or **inner man,** is already being built up by God.

We must, however, be careful not to impose modern ideas of evolutionary development upon Paul's thinking. Modern evolutionary theory does not imply that nature proceeds only by reserving its noblest creations for the end of a process. A type may suddenly emerge, like *homo sapiens*, who towers above the other creatures because he has the ' capacity to name them,' the power to remember, observe and forecast, and can actually determine the course of further development. Yet such an emergence, or ' increment,' in the evolutionary process can neither prove nor disprove the creative intervention of a living Creator. It affords no more cogent proof of Divine intervention than the whole process itself. God is not best seen in the ' gaps,' which may be gaps only in our own knowledge of nature, not in nature itself. Paul's thinking, however, is Hebrew thinking. He has no idea of applying evolutionary development, in the modern scientific sense, to spiritual progress when he says, **I am prepared for this change by God.** The growth of his **inner man** is at every stage God's creative work. Here Paul represents all New Testament thinking. In the parable, the ' seed growing secretly ' is not a symbol of a gradual process, but of the power or Kingdom (reign) of God, producing such comparatively great results as a full head of ripening grain, from apparently small and powerless beginnings. This is the result of God's creative power, or ' reign,' at work ' secretly.' The same idea applies to Paul's doctrine of an **inner man** daily renewed, and of personal immortality as the climax. Eternal Life is in the end, both in Paul and in the other New Testament writers, regarded as a free and royal gift of God's grace, not as the inevitable result of a spiritual process in a good man's life. It is at this point that theories of ' conditional immortality ' are most vulnerable. The New Testament emphasis is upon the creative and redemptive activity of God at every stage in human progress. Paul here thinks of the ' preparation ' or the renewing of his **inner man** as a series of acts of God. The thought is akin to I Cor. xv. 38, **God gives it a body as He pleases,** where Paul does not speculate further on what we would call the organic connexion between the ' bare ' seed and the ' body ' which it afterwards receives as a head of ripening grain. The ultimate guarantee for personal immortality is the sovereign power and character of God revealed in Christ. **I am confident, 6** says Paul ; confident, that is, in the reality of the **heavenly habitation** or heavenly state of being. It is remarkable that one who says elsewhere, ' To me to live is Christ ' (Phil. i. 21), should also say, **While I reside in the body I am away from 7 the Lord.** Paul defines what is meant in the words in brackets. Dr. Moffatt's translation is illuminating and timely. The A.V. and R.V. renderings have produced a false general antithesis between ' faith ' and ' sight.' **To reside in the body** does not mean that fellowship with Christ is absent, but that it is imperfect. **The life I now live in the flesh I live by faith in the Son of God** (Gal. ii. 20). Yet we have so to live without seeing Him. In our experiences of life here, its trials, perplexities, sufferings, conflicts of loyalties, as we seek to do God's will, we sometimes can see only the next step, sometimes can only guess at the meaning and issue of events, while in our darkest moments we cannot see at all (cf. Job. xxvi. 14). Paul really describes what it means to ' walk in darkness,' and yet ' to trust in the name of the Lord ' (Isa. l. 10).

I would fain get away from the body and reside with the 8 Lord, when ' His servants shall serve Him : and they shall see His face ' (Rev. xxii. 3). He would fain live in that day, when we shall

> hear, know, and say
> What this tumultuous body now denies ;
> And feel, who have laid our groping hands away ;
> And see, no longer blinded by our eyes.[1]

I am eager to satisfy Him. Paul now strikes a note of **9-10** grave moral emphasis. He thinks of service, both here and hereafter, not of mere blissful contemplation. Each man must appear before the **tribunal of Christ.** There we appear **without disguise, each to be requited for what he has done with his body.** Paul once again lays stress upon the value and responsibility which attaches to the present life, as against the inevitable moral consequences of the Hellenistic depreciation of the

[1] Rupert Brooke, *1914 and Other Poems*, p. 36.

body. Paul does not conceive of ' life in the flesh ' as the life of ' a ghost tied to a corpse.' He is here uttering a distinctive article of the Christian faith, not merely reproducing Jewish notions of the Messianic judgment. In his mind is the same ethical emphasis which underlies the clause in the Apostle's Creed, ' I believe in the resurrection of the body,' for which modern thought must find an equally efficient moral substitute, if a serious lacuna in the Catholic faith is to be avoided.

Into the question whether the judgment is conceived as universal, or extending to believers only, it is impossible here to enter. Nowhere does Paul give a clear answer. He speaks elsewhere of God as judging the world (Rom. i. 18 ff., iii. 6). Even angels are to be judged (1 Cor. vi. 3). He speaks of those who are perishing, and of their fate as death (2 Cor. ii. 16); of those who reap destruction (Gal. vi. 8). The remarkable utterance in 1 Cor. vi. 2 f., that the ' saints will judge the world,' implies that Christian morality represents the absolute and final standard by which all humanity is to be judged. Paul nowhere encourages morbid curiosity regarding the fate of the wicked. Throughout his whole treatment of the resurrection and the resurrection body it is clearly the resurrection of believers on which his mind is fixed (1 Cor. xv.).

Paul is eager to satisfy Him in this life also. The prospect of the judgment-seat of Christ affects the quality and motive of present moral action (cf. Gal. vi. 4, 5, 9 ; 2 Cor. i. 14 ; 1 Thess. ii. 19). In 1 Cor. iii. 8-15, Paul assumes that the work of the Christian man, i.e. what he has done with his body, will prove of varying value in God's sight, and that reward will not be uniform. The judgment-seat of Christ is not a shadow cast on the Christian hope, but the only tribunal that preserves the eternal values of human life. Ruskin says that ' true humility is in hoping that angels might sometimes admire *our* work ; not in hoping that we should be able to admire *theirs* '[1]; and elsewhere: ' that we should be able to admire the work of angels seems to me the impertinent idea ; not at all, that they should be able to admire ours.'[2] The principle he lays down for artists holds pre-eminently in Christian ethics. Moral

---

[1] *Ariadne Florentina*, VI., § 189.   [2] *Eagle's Nest*, III., § 53.

obedience is judged complete, or incomplete, not when we compare our conduct with an ideal, however sincere and lofty, which after all is but a tribunal set up in our own consciences. Life must be scrutinized in the light of Christ, the Judge of every man's conscience before God (2 Cor. iv. 2). What a man has done with his body covers the whole range of waking conscious life. It includes our most secret thoughts and purposes, as well as our deeds and words. The coming short of an ideal does not necessarily accuse of sin, but leaves room for self-excusing. To appear without disguise is to be stripped of the excuses we fashion to hide the unfaithfulness of our lives. To be requited may mean, not only chastisement, but that our good, which men have spurned or ignored, will be acknowledged. To be eager to satisfy Christ is at once the condition of true penitence and the only kind of conscience which is no longer at the mercy of what other men think right and good, and can alone sustain Christian motives at the height that marks them off from those of all other ethical systems. Paul's moral life is lived between two worlds, and he feels the whole significance and attraction of both. He is deeply conscious of the large moral and spiritual dimensions of ' life in the flesh.'

v. 11–15 : THE CONSTRAINT OF THE LOVE OF CHRIST

If I ' appeal to the interests of men,' then, it is with the fear of 11 the Lord before my mind. What I am is plain to God without disguise, plain also, I trust, to your own conscience. This is not ' recommending myself to you again ' ; it is 12 giving you an incentive to be proud of me, which you can use against men who are proud of externals instead of the inward reality. ' I am beside myself,' am I ? Well, that 13 is between myself and God. I am ' sane,' am I ? Well, 14 that is in your interests ; for I am controlled by the love of Christ, convinced that as One has died for all, then all 15 have died, and that He died for all in order to have the living live no longer for themselves but for Him who died and rose for them.

11   Our translation regards ' appeal to the interests of men ' as
a charge made against Paul. The same charge is cited in
Gal. i. 10. Apparently Paul is accused of telling men in his
preaching what they like to hear. ' If I do so,' he says, ' it is
with the fear of the Lord before my mind.' His work will be
12 judged at no human tribunal. He recurs again to the thought
in iii. 1 ff. In thus reminding his readers of the only light in
which his motives can be regarded as pure, he is not ' recommending' himself, but giving them an opportunity to defend
him against his traducers, and to have a legitimate pride
(cf. i. 14) in one who seeks thus to be judged. His critics pride
themselves on externals, such as their personal knowledge of
Jesus, their relationship with the Jerusalem Church, their
Jewish descent in privilege, perhaps their learning or their elo-
13 quence (cf. x. 1, 10, xi. 22 ff.). Dr. Moffatt's translation of
verse 13 seems hardly to elucidate the difficult connexion of
thought with the context. The charge of madness was no
doubt brought against Paul, but to be sane can scarcely be a
reproach. Paul bids his readers have confidence in his own
sincerity or inward reality, and assume that he is sane. The
words translated, that is in your interests, would then be
rendered, ' that is for you to judge.' If, as his traducers say,
he has ever been beside himself, that is between myself and
God, and does not concern his readers. They have to do with
him in his sane moments. Paul's apostolic call was regarded
by him as much more than an office and authority conferred
upon him. The message he received and the mission on which
he is sent, marked an epoch in the history of God's dealings
with men (cf. iv. 6). Such a claim might well be regarded by
his opponents as pointing to megalomania.

It is also possible that, when Paul speaks of being sane, he
speaks ironically, and actually scores a palpable hit against his
enemies. They have accused him of being able to ' appeal to
the interests of men '—in other words, to get round men by his
fair speech. ' That, surely, is the effort of a man in his right
senses ! ' For any spiritual extravagances connected with his
name he is answerable to God, not to the Corinthians. They
are concerned with those moments when he was sane enough

to ' persuade ' them, or, as his opponents would say, get round them !

The controlling power in his own life is the love of Christ, 14 which means Christ's love towards himself. He seeks to make it the controlling power in his hearers' lives also (verse 18). The word translated controls means ' restrain,' ' take hold of,' or ' grip.' It is the word used by Paul in Phil. i. 23, where he speaks of being ' in a strait betwixt two.' His desires are driven in two directions. In the usage here, movement is possible, but only in one direction—the direction determined by the ' hand ' that grasps him ; the pressure exerted by the dying love of Christ, the climax of a life of complete self-renunciation and selfless service (verse 15). To resist means much more than the repelling of an idea. Active moral resistance is needed in order to thrust aside the appeal of the Cross. The constraint is so strong as to hurt the conscience. Even human heroism and self-sacrifice can lead to the threshold of this Divine constraint. ' Often in the transient lights and shades of conscience we pass on and " know not who it is " ; and not till we see in another the victory that shames our own defeat, and are caught up by an enthusiasm for some realized heroism or sanctity, do the authority of right and the beauty of holiness come home to us as an appeal literally Divine.'[1] Yet, if we are to understand what Paul felt about the Divine self-sacrifice on Calvary, we must travel, with him, immeasurably further than even these magnificent human symbols.

There can be little doubt that the words One has died for all bear a substitutionary meaning, if only the word ' substitution ' could be rescued from some of the connotations which centuries of theological discussion have given it. Paul means that Christ bore voluntarily a doom that should have been ours. Death is the wages of sin, and sin, for Paul, meant resistance to, or inability to do, the will of God, as that will was revealed, not merely as directing outward forms of conduct, but as controlling the inner springs of thought and desire. It

[1] Martineau, *Seat of Authority in Religion*, p. 652 ; cf. H. H. Farmer, *Experience of God*, pp. 30 f.

is well that we should curb our desire to criticize such a substitutionary conception as immoral, until we have understood how inevitable it was that Paul should, after his conversion, put the Cross in the central place in all his system of Christian thinking.

The crucified Messiah in pre-Christian days he hated with all the fervour of a cultivated man who lived in a world where crucifixion was not only suffering, but sheer degradation. ' May the very name of a cross be far removed, not only from the bodies of Roman citizens,' says Cicero, ' but even from their thoughts, their sight, their hearing.'[1] The appearance of the risen Jesus to him on the Damascus road meant that God had raised from the dead this Nazarene felon, and vindicated Him. If it was God's doing, then Paul suddenly felt his whole pre-Christian system of religious thought crash to the ground. He had to find a place for the Cross in a world ruled by God's almighty will. The only way to do so was to regard the death of Jesus as vicarious shame. His former loathing was turned into a passionate and adoring sense of the humiliation undergone by One ' who loved me and gave Himself for me.' The Cross became to him much more than a tragic accident, the work of ' wicked men ' (Acts ii. 23) ; more even than an event that happened according to the ' determinate counsel and foreknowledge of God.' It was an overwhelming revelation of God's own love, displaying, after the manner of love, a loving accountability for the sins of His own creatures. In such a mind as Paul's, where the problem of sin is taken seriously, the barrier between the idea of vicarious doom voluntarily accepted and the idea of loving accountability is very thin.

15 That the dominant note in Paul's thought of the Cross is the overwhelming sense that the Divine heart suffers in and for the sin of the world, and that this Divine suffering is rooted in Divine love, is shown clearly by the words He died for all in order to have the living live no longer for themselves, but for Him who died and rose for them. For Paul, the heart of the Cross is Divine love seeking to win men over to a

[1] *Pro. C. Rabirio,* V. 10.

108

whole-hearted attachment to Christ, who is the 'image of God.' Then all have died to the old life of self-seeking—a real *imitatio Christi*. It is evident that Paul's interest here is also deeply ethical. He has in mind at the moment the charges of self-seeking made against himself, and he is saying that self-seeking cannot live in the heart of one who is controlled by the love of Christ. 'Let this mind be in you which was also in Christ Jesus' conveys the same thought. The words are used by him to introduce a famous passage (Phil. ii. 5-11), which would have been more intelligible if it had been less exploited by the scientific theologian. There are moments when Paul speaks in the mood and temper of a poet. He is speaking here of a vital and transfiguring experience in the lives of men. They become as men who have been 'born again.' They have put off 'the old man,' and put on 'the new man.' They have died and entered upon a life of an entirely new quality ; the living live no longer for themselves. We have become accustomed to the general idea of selflessness as the essence of Christian morality, but there is often a gaping chasm between words and deeds. The realization of it in a human life, or in a community, still bursts upon the world as a surprise, and keeps alive the faith that there is only one source from which it comes. We love, because He first loved us (1 John iv. 19 ; cf. verses 7-18). The Christian Church had to re-mint an old word—*agapē*—in order to convey the new idea. There can be no doubt that in saying here, He died for all, Paul is giving us the vision he himself had of an overwhelming sacrificial love—*the love of Christ*. It controlled, took hold of him with an inescapable grasp, and in it he identified the coercive and creative power of God (ii. 18). Christ not only died, but rose again for men. By His resurrection a new 'Spirit' is given to the world. God's love floods our hearts through the Holy Spirit that has been given us (Rom. v. 5). The love of Christ in thus dying produces a new and unprecedented loyalty to Christ as Lord. By their loyalties the quality of men's lives is determined.

v. 16–21 : The Message of Divine Reconciliation

16 Once convinced of this, then, I estimate no one by what is external ; even though I once estimated Christ by what is

17 external, I no longer estimate Him thus. There is a new creation whenever a man comes to be in Christ ; what is

18 old is gone, the new has come. It is all the doing of the God who has reconciled me to Himself through Christ and has permitted me to be a minister of His reconciliation.

19 For in Christ God reconciled the world to Himself instead of counting men's trespasses against them ; and He entrusted me with the message of His reconciliation. So

20 I am an envoy for Christ, God appealing by me, as it were —be reconciled to God, I entreat you on behalf of Christ.

21 For our sakes He made Him to be sin who Himself knew nothing of sin, so that in Him we might become the righteousness of God.

16 Verse 17 directly carries on the thought of verse 15. In verse 16 we have one of Paul's characteristic parentheses. The thought is suggested by the all died of the previous verse. Their relationship is no longer with the present order of things. They have an entirely new relationship with the exalted Lord. Paul's opponents had been claiming a special authority on the ground of their exclusive knowledge of Christ ' after the flesh '—by which is meant either a personal knowledge, or a close connexion with the original disciples, or some special knowledge of His teaching and His attitude towards the Law. Paul is antagonizing the same men whom he describes in some- what similar terms in verse 12. They evidently repudiated his credentials, inasmuch as he had not known Jesus per- sonally. Paul replies : ' I estimate no one by what is ex- ternal, by the outward circumstances of his life, because all have died. Not even the outward circumstances of the life of Jesus, or His words and deeds, are the foundation of my faith, and the origin of my new life.' The Jesus of Paul is He who died and rose again and, as Lord, is alive for evermore.

THE 'CHRIST AFTER THE FLESH'

Varying interpretations have been given of this verse.

(1) There has been a good deal of discussion as to whether the words rendered by Dr. Moffatt—**even though I once estimated Christ by what is external**—(*though we have known Christ after the flesh*—A.V.) are sufficient to warrant the belief that Paul had actually seen Jesus in the days of His flesh. J. Hope Moulton says that Paul 'was in Jerusalem during that central week of human history, and it was then that he became humanly acquainted with Christ.' Johannes Weiss held the same view.[1] Is it likely, however, that Paul would have set against his opponents' claim to have known Jesus personally, or to have a first-hand knowledge of His life and teaching, what must have been, if it is a fact, only a fleeting glimpse while he was a student in Jerusalem at the school of Gamaliel. The same argument applies, even if he had been present at the trial. Paul would not have used the strong and emphatic word 'know' (=*estimated*) of his relation to Jesus under these circumstances.

(2) Paul's words, ' a Christ after the flesh,' have also been interpreted as meaning a non-spiritual Jewish conception of the Messianic ideal. But this does not suit the context. The whole reference is obviously to the historical person, Jesus Christ. 'Christ' is almost always used by Paul as a proper name. Moreover, it would involve the supposition that Paul, after his conversion, had begun by preaching Christ in a Judaistic fashion. Nothing can be more certain than that, after his conversion, Paul preached the risen and exalted Jesus—a conception quite antagonistic to any known Jewish Messianic idea. A Judaistic phase in his life is unthinkable in view of Gal. i. 15–17.

(3) The refusal to ' *estimate* ' Christ by **what is external**—' to know ' a Christ after ' the flesh '—means that the sayings and doings of Jesus of Nazareth, however well known to and authoritative for Paul they must have been, possessed a religious and credal value, subordinate to the ' revelation '

[1] Cf. C. A. Anderson Scott, *Christianity according to St. Paul*, p. 12.

(Gal. i. 15) of the dying, risen, and exalted Jesus, and the instruction given to Paul by the ' Spirit.' ' The Lord is the Spirit ' (iii. 17). This is the preferable interpretation. It is remarkable how some of Paul's parentheses, such as this verse, are laden with significance for the story of the development of the Christian faith. This refusal to be fettered by the mere example and even words of Jesus exercised a permanent and distinctive influence on New Testament thought. It delivered Christianity from legalism. The tendency represented by Paul's opponents in this letter, and in Galatians, was to quote the example and teaching of Jesus, particularly His attitude towards Jewish institutional religion, in favour of imposing the Jewish Law on the Gentile world, as an essential of Christian faith and practice. By concentrating faith on the exalted Christ, Paul secured that the Christian faith was seen to transcend all temporal and racial limitations. It was stripped of these, ' not by academic analysis, but by the mightier logic of events, and the movement of world-history.'[1] This movement was catastrophic, not evolutionary. A new age had dawned.[2] In refusing to make Jesus of Nazareth the hero of a tradition, Paul conserved the power that would perpetuate that tradition as a living faith. The story of the life on earth is told in the Gospels by those who were worshippers of Jesus before they were His biographers. There were elements in the self-consciousness of Jesus of Nazareth which could be apprehended only by men to whom He had become a living and reigning Lord. No deeper misunderstanding of the tradition in the Gospels could be encouraged than by regarding Paul as having overlaid the historic personality and simpler faith and teaching of Jesus, as described in the Gospels, with theological speculation. The gospel story is not a corrective of theological speculation, but a proof that Christianity is an historical religion, and has its source in the creative personality of Jesus.

It is, I think, possible to trace a movement in New Testament thought, necessitated by the Pauline doctrine of an exalted Lord and also fostered by it, which seeks to give the

---

[1] B. W. Bacon, *Jesus and Paul*, p. 57.   [2] See notes on verse 17.

human life of Jesus an increasingly commanding place in the Christian message. The Pauline mission preceded the publication of the Synoptic Gospels, and we have also the extraordinarily realistic picture of the human struggle and temptations of Jesus, meant to fit Him for the Great High Priesthood, in the Epistle to the Hebrews. Not Paul, but Paulinism, may have tended to obscure the origin of the Christian faith in an historical personality. This is not to deny the influence, powerful and dominating from the first, of the material collected in the sources which lie behind the Synoptic Gospels ; nor does it deny Paul's own full knowledge of Jesus' life and teaching. The tendency would be to give to the human life a merely docetic significance, in the light of the firm conviction that the resurrection had proved Christ to be a Divine Being. This whole movement of credal revaluation of the ministry on earth reaches its climax in the anti-docetic emphasis of the Johannine Gospel and Epistles.[1]

There is a new creation whenever a man comes to be in Christ. Dr. Moffatt's translation brings out the full significance of the words. Paul here defines more clearly than anywhere else the content of the phrase so often used by him— he condition of being ' in Christ.' This condition is the being in a ' new world,' a ' new creation.' The movement of history is conceived by Paul as catastrophic. He accepts the Jewish doctrine of the two ' ages ' or ' aeons '—the present age, this world (Gal. i. 4 ; 1 Cor. ii. 6), under the sway of the evil powers (2 Cor. iv. 4 ; Eph. vi. 12), and ' the world to come ' (Eph. i. 21 ; Luke xviii. 30). Here Paul not only makes use of the language of current Jewish thinking, but of the teaching of Jesus Himself regarding the Kingdom of God. Paul regards the ' Kingdom,' or ' new age,' as already present for the believer ' in Christ.' The power of the ' world to come ' is already in his life. We may compare Jesus' words in Luke xi. 20. He regarded the Kingdom as both present in His own person and

17

---

[1] I have here made considerable use of some pages from my book, *The Historic Jesus in the New Testament*, where the movement of credal revaluation of the earthly life of Jesus is developed in more detail.

works, and as future, about to be consummated in His death
and resurrection (Mark xiv. 62 and parallels). Paul shared the
belief of the early Christian Church in the imminent ' Appearing ' of Jesus finally to inaugurate His kingdom on earth. At
the same time he is conscious that the power of the Kingdom
is already at work. Of the Christian, the man who is in Christ,
Paul elsewhere says that God ' hath delivered us from the
power of darkness, and hath translated us into the kingdom of His dear Son ' (Col. i. 13, A.V.). It is in terms of
this apocalyptic thinking, which represents the Jewish cos-
mology, that we must understand what it means to be ' in
Christ.' The ' creature ' is new, because the Creation, or world
in which he now moves, is new (Gal. vi. 15). What is old
is gone, the new has come. Paul's words are ' Behold ! the
new has come.' In ' behold ! ' there is a note of triumph, as
though what has happened has happened suddenly, and is a
Divine apocalypse or revelation. The fact of Christ is for
Paul an act of God—God's own creative act for the salvation
of the world. As a revelation given to Paul at his conversion,
it was interpreted by him both as an amazing act of Divine
love and grace towards himself, and as a Divine act, in the
results of which Paul and all Christians are permitted to share.
The modern equivalent for this type of apocalyptic thinking
would be the faith of the Christian man that the universe in
which we live is not a blind mechanism, but is in the end our
ally.

> That one Face, far from vanish, rather grows,
> Or decomposes but to recompose,
> Become my universe that feels and knows.[1]

It is the sphere of Christ's victory over sin and death. Where
the environment is still hostile, we are ' predestined ' to share
Christ's victory, through conflict and by acceptance of the
grace and power of Jesus Christ, the Saviour. To be in Christ
is to be ' saved.' Personal salvation is a symptom and element
of ultimate reality. We know . . . that those who love God,
those who have been called in terms of His purpose, have His

---

[1] Browning, *Dramatis Personae* (Epilogue).

aid and interest in everything.[1] In this ' new creation,' a ' new
world ' that God has brought into being (verse 18), calamity
may come, but it does not separate us from the love of God.
God, not a mere system of ' things,' ' works together ' or co-
operates with the ' saved ' man, for good.

Thoughts like these must accompany us, if we are to in- 18-
terpret the succeeding verses aright. In the preceding verses 19
God's redeeming love is exhibited on an absolute scale, and
affects the whole scheme of things. That revelation also
creates a new situation for the sinful, as between God and
men. It brings reconciliation.

THE DIVINE RECONCILIATION

Paul expressly says that Reconciliation is the act of God—
all the doing of God (v. 18). It is a new and friendly relationship which God initiated and brought into being through
Christ, and replaces an old relationship defined as counting
men's trespasses against them. He indicates much more
than a change of attitude on the human side in response to
a discovery that God is friendly. It is quite true to say that
Paul never speaks of God being reconciled to men ; but he
does say here—to bring out the full meaning of the words—
' that God was engaged in Christ in reconciling the world to
Himself ' (verse 19). (In the A.V., the comma after ' Christ '
is misleading.) There is an active ' Divine aggression ' or
invasion of the estranged human heart. ' No assertion could
be more empty than the Christian saying that God is love, if
that love were simply a subjective disposition on the part of
a being for ever inactive and unseen. If God exists as a good
will, that will must do its work in the world of time and event
as a will to power not wholly unlike our own, and so coming
to itself as we must, through the saving of others. Christianity
is right in holding that such a God, if He exists, must somehow

---

[1] Rom. viii. 28. The A.V. and R.V. renderings express the truth in a
form ' congenial to the " modern mind," which thinks so much of the
universe as an orderly system of laws, and likes to believe that " it will
all come right in the end " ' (C. H. Dodd, *Romans*, p. 138, *q.v.*).

appear in the temporal order.'[1] That 'Divine aggression' Paul denotes by 'reconciliation.' Its supreme and final manifestation is the dying and rising again of Jesus (cf. Col. i. 20–22 ; Rom. v. 10 f.).

We cannot begin to sound the depths of Paul's conception of Reconciliation without bearing in mind a kindred Pauline conception. Reconciliation and the 'wrath' of God are inseparably interwoven. It is better, I think, to speak of the 'wrath' rather than of the 'anger' of God.[2] The 'wrath' of God is not mentioned in this chapter ; but it must be in the background if we are to see, in these verses, as I think we must, Paul's expression of what he regarded as the essential meaning of the Cross of Christ. To speak of God's 'anger' is to suggest an anthropopathic idea. But there is a quality in the Divine wrath, as Paul interprets it, which transcends the frailer human passion, and is necessarily absent from even the noblest human indignation against wrong.

The conception is much more than a fierce anthropopathism. What we call the moral consequences of sin, Paul thought of as the direct result of the judicial action of a living, personal God. He assumes that we live in a moral order of things which is our continual environment. To Paul, that moral order is equivalent to the will of God. To sin against it does not involve that certain moral consequences are automatically set in motion. God is in them all. They are at all points determined by His will. That these consequences sometimes fall on innocent lives, means that our moral order is such that, being persons, our lives are personally entangled, for good or for evil. These consequences may be physical, or they may issue in conscious or unconscious estrangement from God ; certainly in injury to character. Yet they are not impersonal. God is in control. He is not only a living God who acts, but a God who 'activates,' to use an obsolescent word. His wrath and His love are alike His Word, which does not return into Him 'void.' This word of God is the source of

---

[1] W. E. Hocking, *Human Nature and its Remaking*, p. 399.
[2] Dr. C. H. Dodd (Moffatt Commentary on Rom. i. 18) also would retain 'wrath.'

the moral consequences of doing evil, and has itself a redemptive significance. The wrath of God is the active manifestation of his essential incapacity to be morally indifferent, and to let evil alone.

The wrath of God is an integral constituent of His love. Otherwise Paul would not say that it was 'revealed from heaven' (Rom. i. 18). Any real difficulty there is in accepting the wrath of God as a moral factor in His dealings with men, we cannot but trace to a non-moral conception of love. Divine love is also Divine goodness. No love can be called good which lacks the capacity for instinctive repulsion, in the presence of the mean and the base. Such a lack belongs not to a man's virtues, but to his vices. We do no wrong to God's essential and holy love when we assent to that inevitable Divine reaction against sin, which, so unlike our own, is free from the imperfection and infirmity that lie in wait for an angry man. Holy love alone makes such an attitude to human sin possible, as Paul describes by the Divine wrath. 'The behaviour of Jesus in the Gospels and our own highest experiences indicate as much. It is love alone that makes wrath pure, sublime, redemptive.'[1]

Paul expresses the view that the wrath and the redemptive love of God (or 'righteousness' of God) are one Divine activity by saying that both are revealed (Rom. i. 17 f.). God alone reveals. The Divine activity of **reconciliation** is Paul's finest and noblest expression of the love of God, and necessarily includes both conceptions. He does not stay at this point in this particular letter to theorize—if he ever does theorize—as to the connexion of redemption with the Cross. He simply states it, in all its naked and profoundly moving reality, in verse 21. Discussion as to whether the 'reconciliation' is on God's part, or only on ours, or on both, is merely fruitless and irrelevant. By so doing we only drag the Pauline idea of **reconciliation** down into a sphere—the human sphere—where it does not belong. The Divine reconciliation is one complete activity of Divine love, and does what only God

[1] H. R. Mackintosh, *The Christian Experience of Forgiveness*, p. 210 ; to whom I am also indebted in the preceding sentences.

can do. We 'receive' (A.V.) reconciliation, in order that
there may be a change in our own attitude towards God.
(Rom. v. 11). Estrangement from God is infinitely more
serious than a tragic misunderstanding on man's part. The
latter interpretation, in its turn, carries with it an inadequate
view of the place which human sinning has in the Divine heart.
It would inevitably come to mean that we are such ' insects '
in God's sight that it does not *really* matter to Him what we
do.[1] Human estrangement from God has its objective counterpart in the Divine heart—not a weaker counterpart, with less
moral content than the sense of guilt has in a man's conscience.
The very sense of estrangement has its Divine origin, if the conception of the 'wrath' of God is a true one. 'Wrath' and 'love'
are one Divine activity, which Paul here calls ' reconciliation.'
Together they are the complete response of Divine love to the
tragic fact that men whom God created and loves, have become what they are through sinning. The essence of the faith
of Paul, and of the New Testament, including the Gospels, is
that God is stirred to the depths of His Being by the condition
of men. A repentant soul is one of those exalted and wonderful happenings into which ' angels ' desire to look and, having
seen it, rejoice (Luke xv. 10 ; cf. Matt. xviii. 14). Is this
Divine heart-beat not what we hear beneath the simpler, yet
whole-hearted, excitement of the characters in the three para-
bles of Luke xv. ? Does Paul not share ' the mind that was
in Christ Jesus ' when he beseeches his readers, as he does
in verse 20, to be reconciled to God ? For this message, the
living presence of Christ is as truly essential as it is when we
say that, without the presence of Jesus and His voice as He
spoke of the Lost Son, the parable would be emptied of all
Divine meaning and guarantee. Paul feels this. It is an
essential part of his message when he says, **I am an envoy
for Christ, God appealing by me, as it were—be reconciled to
God, I entreat you on behalf of Christ.**

[1] ' If the Atonement . . . simply means the clearing up of a misunderstanding, this certainly leaves us in the dark as to how far it would really
matter if this misunderstanding were not cleared up ' (E. Brunner, *The
Mediator*, p. 489).

Nowhere else than in this Reconciliation passage does Paul make it more evident that his own conversion experience is the real origin of all his thinking. Note the substitution of me for ' us ' in Dr. Moffatt's translation : **He entrusted me.** At the same time, it must not be forgotten that the Pauline gospel of reconciliation also includes reconciliation on the Christian's part to his environment of men and things. It includes ' the promise of sitting in the heavenly places amid the tumult of the present hour.'[1] This aspect of reconciliation is itself no dream, no 'pathetic fallacy,' no pleasing shadow cast by our own longings or momentary experience upon the rough-nesses of our environment. It is **God's peace, that surpasses all our dreams** (Phil. iv. 7). Peace with God is peace with men, and also the assured faith that even when things are against us we are held securely by His love, and aided by His invincible grace and power. Reconciliation is a personal rela-tionship with God, conferred of grace by God Himself. There-fore, it necessarily involves that no man can have the grace of God in his heart, and deny its working reality in the world that God has made and governs, with all its vicissitudes, in which He has appointed us to live. This reconciliation with our environment is as far as possible removed from the Stoic resignation—' the retreat of the tortoise into its shell,' as it has been called. Reconciliation is not an affair of the reason, but of that nobler reason we call faith. We reason from the standpoint of what we already know of God, who permits trouble to approach and darkness to descend upon us. Recon-ciliation may be described, in its issues for life and conduct, as ' the nobly ethical attitude to affliction, which does not merely safeguard moral good already won against degrada-tion, as the Stoic resignation may do, but makes trouble itself the direct means to further enrichment.'[2] Reconciliation means more than the refusal to complain and the cultivation of fortitude. It means a faith that God has something more to tell us about life and to give us in life than He has yet given. Not to the mere philosopher, but to the Christian man, in his

[1] J. Oman, *Grace and Personality*, 3rd ed., p. 126.
[2] A. E. Taylor, *The Faith of a Moralist*, I., p. 154.

Christlike ' meekness,'[1] is given the power so to deal with the earth, its trials and mysteries, as to inherit it.

20   Paul, who has been made **a minister of his reconciliation,** now speaks, charged with the imperial authority of an ambassador or **envoy for Christ.** This authority, however, is expressed not by a command, but by an entreaty, which is the
21 Divine method ; **God appealing by me.** At the heart of this appeal is the cost of it. He ,made Him to be sin who Himself knew nothing of sin. Much confusion is caused in our minds by the way in which we interpret God **made Him,** as though it meant God ' compelled Him,' or ' demanded of Him.' In Hebrew thought, all that happens is regarded as happening within the sphere of God's sovereign power, while the personal responsibility and freedom of the human agent are maintained (cf. 2 Sam. xxiv. 1, 10). To forget this mode of thinking is to introduce much unnecessary theological perplexity into Paul's words here. All that Christ did, Paul regards as done voluntarily, in accordance with the Divine will. Paul would have assented to the Johannine utterance, ' I and the Father are one ' (literally, ' a unity ' ; John x. 30). The unity is not merely a metaphysical unity, but a unity of will and purpose. We have no more right to interpret Paul's words here as meaning that God has somehow to be induced to love men, than we have the right to say to a mother, bearing her child's sin on a loving heart, that she is thereby being induced to love her child. God gives the pure and loving heart, all the more sensitive in proportion as it is pure and loving. Such a heart cannot be at a distance from the child's shame and sin, but identifies itself instinctively with these. It becomes that shame and sin. *Mitschuld ist viel mehr als Mitleid.* The shame becomes an element in the personality of the mother, even more really than it is yet an element in the self of the erring child. The child who has sinned may feel the shame even less, in proportion as the sin has alarmed him. ' The conscious haunting presence of the sin is a paralyzing, not an intensifying, of the power of penitence. The penitence of the child may be fiercer

[1] See notes on x. 1.

and wilder; but it is, in comparison, shallow, mixed, impotent, unreal.'[1] The mother ' becomes ' the sin of her child, just in proportion as she ' knows ' no such sin in her own experience.

It is also for the reason that the sin first becomes, as it were, the mother's sin, that there is hope that the child may acknowledge it in true penitence. Similarly, when Paul says that God **made Him to be sin who Himself knew nothing of sin,** he is emphasizing the appropriate *inwardness* of the connexion between such a Bearer and such a burden (cf. Gal. iii. 13). So complete is the inwardness that when Christ applies to Himself the prophetic words, ' He was numbered with the transgressors ' [*classed among the criminals*] (Luke xxii. 37), he speaks neither in reproach nor in resentment, but in a compassionate mood of deep silent agreement with God. Christ in the sympathy of love entered into the whole condition and responsibilities of sinful men. He entered as far as love that **knew nothing of sin** can go, which is all the way. Paul assumes what we are most unfortunately compelled to call the ' sinlessness ' of Jesus ; for ' sinlessness ' is a negative term. It must stand for the idea of the complete moral supremacy and spotless purity of Him who knew temptation, but never yielded. When Paul says that Christ **knew nothing of sin,** he was not merely safeguarding the character of Jesus, but describing that positive quality of the Divine love which, because it is sinless love, has a sense of complete loving accountability for the sinner. ' Vicariousness is only another name for love ' (Bushnell). Similarly it is God's loving purpose that, through the realization of what sin is to Christ, we may enter into a new inward relation to the will or ' righteousness of God,' **that in Him we might become the righteousness of God.** Nothing in our new personality, no thought or action, is unrelated to the fact that we are thus ' reconciled ' or forgiven. We become actual embodiments of God's saving power, or **righteousness.**

It cannot be stated too emphatically that not merely the Pauline but the whole New Testament conception of the relation of Christ to human sin must remain unintelligible, and

[1] R. C. Moberly, *Atonement and Personality*, p. 122.

even repulsive, to those who take an ultimately humanistic view of the Person of Jesus. The New Testament view now stands or falls by its correspondence or otherwise with the facts of Jesus' own self-consciousness, as they emerge in the Gospels. In words like those of Mark x. 45, or Matt. xxvi. 28, we already encounter the realities which emerge in the earliest Christian thought as a doctrine of reconciliation through the suffering and death of Jesus. The Jesus of the Gospels is already the bearer and depositary of the Divine character and purpose which is regarded as underlying all history and all human life.

vi. 1–13 : THE MARKS OF THE TRUE MINISTER OF GOD

vi.

1 I appeal to you too, as a worker with God, do not receive the
2 grace of God in vain. (He saith,

> *I have heard you in the time of favour,*
> *and helped you on the day of salvation.*

3 Well, here is *the time of favour*, here is *the day of salvation*.)
I put no obstacle in the path of any, so that my ministry
4 may not be discredited ; I prove myself at all points a true
minister of God, by great endurance, by suffering, by
5 troubles, by calamities, by lashes, by imprisonment ;
6 mobbed, toiling, sleepless, starving ; with innocence,
insight, patience, kindness, the holy Spirit, unaffected
7 love, true words, the power of God ; with the weapons of
integrity for attack or for defence, amid honour and dis-
8 honour, amid evil report and good report, an ' impostor '
9 but honest, ' unknown ' but well-known, *dying* but here
I am *alive, chastened but not killed*, grieved but always
10 glad, a ' pauper,' but the means of wealth to many, without a penny but possessed of all.
11 O Corinthians, I am keeping nothing back from you ; my *heart*
12 *is wide open* for you. ' Restraint ' ?—that lies with you,
13 not me. A fair exchange now, as the children say ! Open
your hearts wide to me.

Here is a passage which gains immensely in significance, as compared with the A.V. and the R.V., by the substitution of ' I ' for ' we.'[1] The sense of ambassadorship still possesses the 1 writer. He appeals to the Corinthians, **as a worker with God,** with a Divine mission, not **to receive the grace of God in vain.** He cites a passage from Isa. xlix. 8. (Septuagint version) about 2 God receiving men into favour, or ' reconciling ' them. The passage originally refers to the mission of the Servant of the Lord, which includes the Gentiles. Paul makes use of it in order to drive home his argument that, in Jesus Christ, God is absolutely and decisively present in redeeming power. This final reconciliation is an era of grace. It is *the time of favour.* The ' now ' of the A.V. is rightly rendered here. Paul does not mean ' now or never,' but emphasizes that the era that has been promised is now come. The nature of the **new creation** has been already described in the preceding verses, and men must not treat it casually.

The connexion of these verses with what goes before is not $^{3-}_{10}$ at once obvious. Paul's argument often feels rather than thinks its way.[2] Here he feels instinctively that his ministry will **be discredited,** if the lives of his friends at Corinth do not 3 show its fruits. He reminds them that his own manner **of** life as a **true minister of God** puts no **obstacle in the path,** preventing anyone from *living* the gospel. The apparent 4 egotism is explicable, as he goes on to describe again his physical sufferings and troubles, and the attacks on his character. These he has been enabled to survive, not in his own strength, but by the power of God. He has employed **the weapons of integrity** (see verse 6), the only weapons he 7 had **for attack or for defence.** The rhythmical form reappears, $^{8-}_{10}$ as it usually does when Paul begins to speak of those startling contrasts of which his life is full (cf. xi. 23-28). Paul gives

---

[1] p. xxxv.

[2] *Oblique vero et quasi per cuniculos latenter incedens.* Thus Jerome, in his *Preface to the Galatians,* describes Paul's thought as ' moving indirectly, and as one might say, unobserved, through underground passages.' Although Jerome's remark is connected with his peculiar theory of the dispute with Peter (Gal. ii. 11 ff.) (viz. that it was a dispute arranged for purposes of edification), his words aptly describe a certain aspect of Paul's style.

noble expression to the thought that the nobler and more devoted the servant of God, the wider is his experience of men, both at their best and at their worst. Both praise and blame, ignominy and honour, reverence and scorn, response and indifference, have been Paul's lot.

11-13   Paul becomes conscious that in the language he has just used his heart has been ' heaved into his mouth.' He pleads, half playfully, that the readers should open their hearts wide to him. A fair exchange now, as the children say! The subordinate clause might be rendered ' as I might say to children.' Let them once for all drop unworthy suspicion and ' restraint.'

vi. 14–vii. 1. A Fragment from a Lost Letter (see pp. 3–6)

vii. 2–7 : God's Comforters are Men

vii.

2 Make a place for me in your hearts ; I have wronged no one, ruined no one, taken advantage of no one.

3 I am not saying this to condemn you. Condemn you ? Why, I repeat, you are in my very heart, and you will be there in

4   death and life alike. I have absolute confidence in you, I am indeed proud of you, you are a perfect comfort to me, I am overflowing with delight, for all the trouble I

5   have to bear. For I got no relief from the strain of things, even when I reached Macedonia ; it was trouble at every turn, wrangling all round me, fears in my own mind.

6   But the God who comforts the dejected comforted me by

7   the arrival of Titus. Yes, and by more than his arrival, by the comfort which you had been to him ; for he gave me such a report of how you longed for me, how sorry you were, and how eagerly you took my part, that it added to my delight.

2   The theme of vi. 13 is continued. The charge of having taken advantage of anyone is again referred to in xii. 16–18. It is impossible to say what exactly is meant by ruined no one. Paul ' might be said to have ruined people who had had

124

to abandon lucrative but unchristian pursuits. The Judaizers declared that his doctrine of Christian freedom was thoroughly immoral ; and some of his disciples, who misinterpreted his teaching, gave the freedom an unchristian and immoral meaning ' (Plummer). Paul only now returns to the subject 3-6 just touched upon in ii. 13, where he breaks away in a paean of praise, and has no time to tell for what he is thankful. He takes time now, and his description here of the lifting of the weight from his heart owing to the news brought by Titus, is evoked by that mutual **confidence** which has been re-established, and has already made itself felt in vi. 1–13, vii. 2. These contrasted moods—the feeling of **the strain of things, trouble at every turn** giving place to **overflowing delight,** and **absolute confidence**—indicate that love such as Paul showed to his fellows is not one passion, but ' a compound of them all.' It has also a certain antiseptic quality which eliminates selfish resentment or the bearing of a grudge. It is **always slow to expose, always eager to believe the best, always hopeful, always patient** (1 Cor. xiii. 7). These verses reveal the depth of the friendship which Paul loved to share with his converts, and the abiding-place which they have in his heart after the storm-clouds of recrimination and rebuke have left the sky.

Paul's genius both for making and for keeping personal 7 friends was one of his outstanding characteristics. The messengers who travel over land and sea for him, enduring much hardship, were proud and glad to do so. Titus must have found it easy and congenial to work for one who, in the midst of his own ' overflowing delight,' appreciates so warmly the service he has done. Titus' heart must have glowed as he heard Paul say that God had sent him as a messenger of comfort to a dejected man, and that the reception Paul's messenger had received at Corinth was a kindness done to Paul himself. Notice also how swift Paul is to acknowledge the sympathetic insight of Titus shown in the terms of the message he delivered. He has told not only the bare facts of the welcome changes at Corinth, but has taken pains to mention **how you longed for me, how sorry you were, and how eagerly you took my part,** and so added to my delight. Paul returns to the subject of Titus in verses 13–16, and in viii. 16–17.

vii. 8–13 : THE DIVINE MINISTRY OF PAIN

8 In fact, if I did pain you by that letter, I do not regret it. I did regret it when I discovered* that my letter had pained
9 you even for the time being, but I am glad now—not glad that you were pained but glad that your pain induced you to repent. For you were pained as God meant you to be
10 pained, and so you got no harm from what I did ; the pain God is allowed to guide ends in a saving repentance never to be regretted, whereas the world's pain ends in
11 death. See what this pain divine has done for you, how serious it has made you, how keen to clear yourselves, how indignant, how alarmed, how eager for me, how determined, how relentless ! You have shown in every
12 way that you were honest in the business. So my letter was written to you, not on account of the offender nor for the sake of the injured party, but in order to let you realize
13 before God how seriously you do care for me. That is what comforts me.

8 **I did regret it when I discovered . . . pained you.** Dr. Moffatt's footnote shows how a Greek participle might be turned by a copyist's slight slip into a present. Scribes were in the habit of using contractions for certain letters. Hort suggested that originally the usual contraction for the Greek letter *ν*, a waved line, was placed above the ω (thus $\tilde{ω}=ων$). The waved line was omitted in certain manuscripts, owing, it may be, to a copyist's imperfect sight, or insufficient light, or simply careless reading. Thus in our extant manuscripts the reading is βλέπω (' I see '), instead of βλέπων (' seeing '). The fact that the Vulgate Latin version renders by a participle is the only indication we have that a manuscript existed with the second reading. This textual

---

* Reading βλέπων with the Vulgate, which ' alone has preserved the true reading, ω̃ being read as ω ' (Hort).

emendation makes the meaning plain, in contrast with the A.V. and R.V. renderings, which are confused in meaning and strangely punctuated. **My letter had pained you.** The question of the ' painful letter ' has been dealt with in the Introduction (pp. xvi. ff.). Among the many lights shed on Paul's personality by this letter, none is more humanly interesting than the fact that even he could sometimes have misgivings about a letter after it is sent.

Paul distinguishes two kinds of ' sorrow ' or **pain. The**[9-10] **pain God is allowed to guide** is a suggestive paraphrase of the words translated in the A.V. ' godly sorrow.' This kind of pain leads to **saving repentance ;** the world's pain **ends in death.** Paul was a great religious psychologist. It may at first sight surprise us that he should thus open up the old sore and seek to analyse the past. But our first impression soon gives way to another, when we realize that he speaks as one who is again on terms of **absolute confidence** with those from whom he was once estranged. Paul, as well as the Corinthians, learned some lessons through the **pain** that had been caused to both. Bygones should be bygones, but it is a mark of complete restoration of mutual confidence when friends who have been estranged are able to talk of some painful experience which God has been **allowed to guide.** Paul, at least, is sure that there are no hidden sparks beneath the ashes which might be revived in the hearts of his readers. If he was over-confident— perhaps he was—at least he has given us some sharply illuminating and deeply searching words on Christian repentance. It is not in order to promote, but because he believes he is in the presence of an example of, true repentance, that he writes. There is a momentous distinction between ' godly sorrow for sin ' and the ' sorrow of the world.' Sins may find us out, and all that may happen is that we are deeply conscious of the pain and loss inflicted on ourselves, or perhaps, though not so poignantly, on others also. Yet there may be no real sense of wrong done. If the loss or pain caused by the exposure could have been prevented, we would not have grieved. Only our pride has been hurt, perhaps our confidence in ourselves shaken or even shattered. We have lost self-respect. We curse ourselves as fools. We blame our nature or our circumstances. This kind of sorrow may pass, but its results remain in spiritual death. There is a 'waft of death' even in such specious and half-hearted apologies as ' I do not profess to be a saint.' The man who so speaks really denies that moral obliquity matters. He has fallen into that habit of moral self-disparagement which marks some peculiarly vain people. ' The sorrow that ends in death hangs in funeral weeds over the sepulchres of the past. Yet the present does not become more wise. Not one resolution is made more firm, nor one habit more holy. Grief is all.'[1] Godly sorrow works **saving repentance.** This kind of repentance is **never to be regretted,** because it produces certain abiding redemptive results, a real change of life, and a permanent alteration of habit. It is ' godly,' or rather ' towards God,' and not only involves a sense that what has been done is a wrong against God, but is also an experience of the way in which God deals with a man who is in the wrong. The wrong deed is the fruit of some evil impulse, which is part of ourselves. Not only part, but in a real sense the whole of ourselves. The confession is made : ' I did it ' ; ' I said it.' ' Repentance, like every religious act, concerns the three cardinal modes of being conscious—knowing, feeling, willing. Sin is recognized, it is disliked, it is disowned. Recognition of sin by itself is not repentance ; it may be defiance. Nor is sorrow for sin repentance, if it be alone in the mind ; it may be remorse or despair. Abandonment of sin, by itself, may be no more than prudence. The regenerating fact is all three, as a unity, baptized in a sense of God's personal grace to the sinful.'[2]

II The creative nature of God's forgiveness of the penitent man is further described. Divine forgiveness means actual transformation of the sordid material of the wrong done into moral gain. It produces qualities of life and character which Paul goes on to mention. **Keen to clear yourselves**—that is, of any further desire to condone the action of the **offender,** or to make excuses for themselves ; indignant—presumably at the

[1] F. W. Robertson, *Sermons : Third Series,* pp. 104 ff.
[2] H. R. Mackintosh, *The Christian Experience of Forgiveness,* p. 234.

shame brought on the Church ; **alarmed**—a more sensitive faculty of ' spiritual alarm,' or, in other words, a conscience more fully awake to what displeases God ; **eager for me**—not merely as a man, but as an apostle of Jesus Christ ; **determined** to uphold the distinction between right and wrong ; **relentless**—allowing no sentimentality to interfere with vindication of the moral law. **The injured party** is Paul him- 12 self. The **offender** was someone who had insulted and fostered disloyalty to Paul's apostolic authority. It is the recognition of that authority,[1] expressed in the words, **realize before God . . . care for me**, which is the crowning result of the ' painful letter.'

vii. 13–16 : A Glimpse of the Heart of Titus

And over and above my personal comfort, I was specially 13
delighted at the delight of Titus. You have all set his
mind at rest. I told him of my pride in you, and I have 14
not been disappointed. No, just as all I have had to say
to you has been true, so all I said about you to Titus, all
my pride in you, has also proved true. His own heart goes 15
out to you all the more when he remembers how you all
obeyed him, and how you received him with reverence and
trembling. I am glad to have full confidence in you. 16

These verses are an overflow from the mood of verses 3–7. **Delighted at the delight of Titus.** ' Friendship redoubleth 13 joys and cutteth griefs in halves. For there is no man that imparteth his joys to his friend, but he joyeth the more ; and no man that imparteth his griefs to his friend, but he grieveth the less.'[2]

With reverence and trembling. Paul tells us that he himself 15 began his work at Corinth **in weakness and fear and with great trembling** (1 Cor. ii. 3). In Eph. vi. 5 the same mood is opposed to ' eye-service.' The **reverence and trembling** are not directed towards Titus, but aroused by their quickened sense of Christian responsibility before God, after all that happened, ' in the

---

[1] Cf. p. xxx.   [2] Bacon, *Essays*, XXVII.

same spirit with which a young man of character would work who was starting in business on capital advanced by a friend ' (Denney). That the Corinthians are said to have received Titus in this way, may mean that Paul's own short and ' painful ' visit, and his abrupt departure, had, after all, left an impression.

viii. 1–15 : THE GRACE OF LIBERALITY AND ITS DIVINE ORIGINATOR

viii.

1 Now, brothers, I have to tell you about the grace God has given

2 to the churches of Macedonia. Amid a severe ordeal of trouble, their overflowing joy and their deep poverty

3 together have poured out a flood of rich generosity ; I can testify that up to their means, aye and beyond their means,

4 they have given—begging me of their own accord, most urgently, for the favour of contributing to the support of

5 the saints. They have done more than I expected ; they gave themselves to the Lord, to begin with, and then (for so God willed it) they put themselves at my disposal.

6 This has led me to ask Titus to complete the arrangements for the same gracious contribution among yourselves, as

7 it was he who started it. Now then, you are to the front in everything, in faith, in utterance, in knowledge, in all zeal, and in love for us*—do come to the front in this gracious enterprise as well. I am not issuing any orders, only using the zeal of others to prove how sterling your

9 own love is. (You know how gracious our Lord Jesus Christ was ; rich though He was, He became poor for the sake of you, that by His poverty you might be rich.) But

10 I will tell you what I think about it ; it is to your interest to go on with this enterprise, for you started it last year, you were the first not merely to do anything but to want

11 to do anything. Now, carry it through, so that your readiness to take it up may be equalled by the way you

* Reading ἐξ ὑμῶν ἐν ἡμῖν with א C D G, almost all the evidence of the Latin and Syriac versions, etc.

carry it through—so far as your means allow. If only
one is ready to give according to his means it is acceptable ; 12
he is not asked to give what he has not got. This does not 13
mean that other people are to be relieved and you to
suffer : it is a matter of give and take ; at the present 14
moment your surplus goes to make up what they lack,
in order that their surplus may go to make up what you
lack. Thus it is to be give and take—as it is written,   15

He who got much had nothing over,
and he who got little had not too little.

THE COLLECTION FOR THE SAINTS

Chapters viii. and ix. form a distinct section of the Epistle.
They deal with a subject which is raised in 1 Cor. xvi. 1–4,
and clearly could not have been resumed until the strained
relationship had been completely removed and mutual confidence restored (vii. 16). Paul goes on to speak of the fund
which he was raising in all the Gentile-Christian communities
on behalf of the poor belonging to the Church at Jerusalem.
In Acts xxiv. 17, and Rom. xv. 25, the destination of the
money is mentioned. At an earlier date, there had been a
famine in Judea, and Paul and Barnabas had taken to
Jerusalem a contribution from Antioch (Acts xi. 29). The
same circumstances are referred to in Gal. ii. 10. The particular situation which made the collection necessary is nowhere stated. It is probable that a large majority of the
members and adherents of the Jerusalem Church would
naturally spring from the poorer classes. It was to these that
Jesus himself chiefly appealed. Few would join the Christian
Church, in that Jewish ecclesiastical centre, from the ranks
of the *élite*, wealthy, or well-to-do. Moreover, greater demands
would be made on the generosity of this Church than were
made on other Christian communities. Crowds of pilgrims
came to Jerusalem, both Jews and Jewish Christians, at the
times of the great feasts. Charity and hospitality would be

needed on these occasions. ' The pilgrims were often poor ; fatigue must have fostered diseases in the crowded city ; food was dear when demand was great and supply limited. Generous charity on the part of the Church in Jerusalem was not merely right and Christian ; it was also wise and prudent, for it was effective in spreading the knowledge of the truth and in conciliating the goodwill of the Jewish strangers who found help and kindness from the Church in their need.'[1] The voluntary self-imposed system of ' communism ' (Acts ii. 44 f.) proved insufficient. It was emotional and unorganized, and circumstances had outgrown it.

This collection would have a peculiar significance in Paul's mind, who regarded it as much more than the meeting of a financial need (cf. chapters viii. and ix. *passim*). From the point of view of the Jerusalem Church there was a religious cleavage between the Jewish-Christian community and the Gentile Church. It must have been difficult to recognize in these upstart Gentile communities, with their absence of any traditional connexion with the Jewish Church, ' fellow-heirs of the promises.' ' The vision of Jehovah's world-wide empire might fill the soul of Paul, as earlier it had filled the soul of Isaiah, but the vision of the prophet is rarely shared in its fullness by the people.'[2] The concordat at Jerusalem did not remove from many minds the unwillingness to share ancestral privileges with Gentiles, thus freely admitted to a Church which was regarded as the continuance of the Church of Israel. The fact that this voluntary assistance came to the Jerusalem Church from Gentile sources must have been a powerful weapon to break down Jewish ancestral prejudice among Jerusalem Christians. No finer example than this contribution could be found of the power and initiative of the Christian faith in thus transcending racial barriers. Quite naturally, Paul asks and expects converts, many of them of a different race and nationality, to come to the aid of the Jerusalem Church.

[1] W. M. Ramsay, *Pictures of the Apostolic Church*, pp. 236 ff.
[2] G. S. Duncan, *St. Paul's Ephesian Ministry*, p. 232. The whole chapter in Professor Duncan's book is very relevant and illuminating.

The Churches of Macedonia. Paul begins by bringing for- 1 ward their example as pioneers in the great work of breaking down racial barriers. Macedonia here does not mean the Roman province, but the ancient kingdom of Macedonia in which Philippi, Thessalonica, and Beroea were situated. Paul speaks 2 of their deep poverty (*lit.*, ' down-to-bottom poverty '). We are told that the Roman government had commandeered the profits from the rich mineral resources of the country, and had also reserved to itself the importation of salt and the felling of timber for building ships.[1] In addition to this permanent drain on economic resources, the poverty of the Macedonian Church must have been increased by persecution and ostracism—a severe ordeal of trouble. It is little wonder that Paul speaks with wonder and admiration of a **flood of rich generosity** which is the result of the meeting of two such strangely mingled streams as overflowing joy and an experience of deep poverty. **More than I expected.** The reference 5 is not merely to a contribution of money. **They gave themselves to the Lord, to begin with**—an act of surrender which brought financial loss and hardship and social ostracism. **They also put themselves at my disposal** (cf. viii. 16 f., ix. 4). ' Luke and Aristarchus, when they travelled with St. Paul to Rome, must have voluntarily passed as his servants ; i.e. as slaves, in order to be admitted to the convoy.'[2] Such self-sacrificing personal service rendered to Paul gives content to the words, **for so God willed it,** as an expression of humble thanksgiving. **Gracious contribution** translates one word, 6 *charis*, or ' grace,' which is also translated **gracious enterprise** in verse 7. The word is used here as indicating that the gifts asked for are in response to the grace God has given, the effect of the Christian message on men's hearts (cf. ix. 15). Paul never uses the ordinary word for collection, as in 1 Cor. xvi. 1, in these chapters. He speaks of it as **the favour of contributing** (verse 4 ; *lit.*, ' the fellowship of serving '), ' an act of munificence ' (viii. 20), a ' blessing ' (ix. 5 ; translated by Dr. Moffatt, **contribution**). The word translated **fund** in

[1] A. Plummer, 2 Corinthians, *I.C.C.*, p. 233.
[2] W. M. Ramsay, *The Letters to the Seven Churches*, p. 33.

verse 19 is also *charis*. Paul uses all the resources of language to dispel any merely commercial atmosphere. He appeals not for a contribution, but to the Christian heart of the contributors.

9 **You know how gracious our Lord Jesus Christ was.** This verse is bracketed as a parenthesis, but it is no mere digression in the thought. When Paul thus reminds his readers of the ' grace of the Lord Jesus Christ,' he strikes the dominant note of his whole appeal. It is a theme never absent from his mind, and has its origin in his own conversion-experience. He himself was the recipient of unspeakable ' grace ' or ' favour ' beyond all deserving, when Christ, whose followers at the moment he was persecuting, revealed to him the place he had in the Divine heart. He thinks of Christ as pre-existent in heaven with God (as the Fourth Evangelist does). He gave up His heavenly existence in order to share the lowly lot of men. It is not literal poverty that Paul means when he writes, **rich though He was, He became poor for the sake of you.** It is incorrect to think of Jesus as having ever endured grinding poverty, such as was known in His own day as in ours. What Paul means is more fully developed in Phil. ii. 5–11. Jesus entered our human life, accepted all its limitations and weaknesses (' took upon Him the form of a servant '), and shrank from nothing, not even death on the cross itself, in order to carry out God's redemptive purpose. Paul's thought here is an interpretation of the self-consciousness of Jesus. While He was on earth, Jesus knew Himself to be a King without a throne, deprived of his rightful place in the hearts of men. ' The Son of Man ' (a title which assumes both Divine origin and a real relationship to men) ' hath not where to lay His head ' (Matt. viii. 20).

THE PRE-EXISTENCE OF CHRIST

Our minds find it difficult to include in the range of our religious thinking the idea of the pre-existence of Christ. For Paul, Jesus is not a supernatural Divine Being because he is pre-existent. He is pre-existent because in Paul's own experience, and in the experience of the Church, Jesus has become 'Lord,' possessing 'the name (or nature) that is above every name.' The assumption of Christ's pre-existence is an inevitable deduction from Paul's conception of the exalted Christ. It is 'the pendant and complement of the resurrection.' So far as we can see, there is no trace of a doctrine of the pre-existence of Jesus in the primitive preaching as described in the opening chapters of the Acts of the Apostles. But Paul's thought moves, under the pressure of his own experience of the risen Christ, to the idea of Christ as the eternal pre-existent Son. Paul speaks of 'one Lord, Jesus Christ, through whom are all things, and we through Him' (I Cor. viii. 6). In this sentence he describes Christ as the pre-existent agent in creation. Paul can conceive of no activity of God in which Christ had no share, because the Divine act of redemption, through Christ, is for him the perfect expression of all Divine activity. If he speaks of Christ as the agent in creation, he speaks first, in the same sentence, of Christ as 'Lord,' the title bestowed on the risen Saviour (Phil. ii. 11). Mighty religion, such as Paul's was, gives rise to mighty speculation.

Jewish doctrines of pre-existence can only partially help us to understand Paul's doctrine of Christ's pre-existence. The Jew had a doctrine of pre-existence which he applied to the great determining factors in his own religion. The Law was pre-existent. Moses on the Mount is shown a 'pattern' of the Tabernacle. What is really intended is that both 'Law' and the Tabernacle with its appointments and ritual are not man-made, nor are they after-thoughts of God Himself. They were in His mind from all eternity. Their eternal existence, however, is not so much pre-existence as *latent* existence, in contrast to the pre-existence of Christ. Paul speaks of the gospel he preached as 'the mystery hid from all ages and generations,' now revealed in Jesus Christ. Of the Christian it is said that **God chose us in Him ere the world was founded** (Eph. i. 4). In other words, that Christ should take possession of men's lives is no mere accident or choice of theirs, but God's eternal purpose for men. When Paul speaks of Christ as

135

pre-existent in heaven, he is making use of a form of thought natural to him, unfamiliar to us, to which he gives a peculiarly Christian content. What he means to convey is truth for all time. All that Christ stands for in the life of the Christian is all that God's eternal gracious purpose can and will do for us. ' Pre-existence, in some sense, must belong to One who is placed on the side of Deity.'[1]

(1) It is essential to note that Paul's primary interest in speaking here of ' the grace our Lord Jesus Christ ' is ethical, not metaphysical. This is well brought out in Dr. Moffatt's paraphrase : **You know how gracious our Lord Jesus Christ was.** The same is true of the Philippians passage, where Paul urges upon his readers, ' Let this mind be in you, which was also in Christ Jesus ' (ii. 5). The ethical example is found in what the older generation of theologians called the ' condescension ' of Jesus ; as in Lyte's hymn, ' familiar, patient, condescending, free.' Unfortunately ' condescend ' is one of our English words that has become debased in meaning. It now suggests an offensive superiority and patronage. ' Before it was spoiled by later usage, it connoted two vital elements in the idea of grace, i.e. generosity and reconciliation. To " condescend," in older English, was a noble action. It meant generally to waive one's rights and claims, or to forgo some privilege for the sake of others. That, and coming to an agreement. Condescension was a genuine favour, the yielding of a higher power or authority to some request, the generous consideration which made strength agree or consent to a plea from weakness.'[2] This older meaning is exactly what Paul means by the ' graciousness ' of Jesus. **Graciousness is a virtue that** ' exalts the dispenser and abashes the recipient.'

(2) It is also most important to note that the cogency of the ethical example, here and in Phil. ii. 5–11, is not merely

---

[1] H. A. A. Kennedy, *Theology of the Epistles*, p. 80. Dr. Kennedy also brings strong reasons to bear against the idea that in his doctrine of the pre-existence of Christ, Paul is making use of the early myth of the ' archetypal man ' which plays a part in Jewish apocalyptic tradition. His doctrine arises immediately out of his experience of ' God in Christ.'

[2] J. Moffatt, *Grace in the New Testament*, pp. 195 ff.

the appeal of Jesus' personal character. Paul, like other early Christian preachers, must have rehearsed narratives of the life of Jesus. It would be a mistake to think that he regarded these as unimportant (cf. notes on v. 18), but in his letters he sees the whole life and death of Jesus in the light of a Divine Being who, being rich in the heavenly glory of a pre-existent state, voluntarily exchanged that life for a state of humanity, became poor by appearing in human form (Phil. ii. 8). This self-sacrificing condescension of Jesus is the visible expression of God's glory in the face of Jesus Christ (iv. 6). The grace of Christ is also the grace of God. The voluntary humiliation of Jesus is an ' apocalypse ' of that self-sacrificing Love which is in the eternal heart of God. Paul thought of Jesus in the days of His flesh, and especially on the closing day of all, as in possession of Divine power and love which he refused to use on His own behalf, but held and exercised only for the benefit of others. To Paul the Cross was an unspeakable condescension, and an ' unspeakable gift.'[1] On the manner of the Incarnation he never speculates. If God is actually what Christ revealed Him to be—a God of Love—His appearing in the world of time is inevitable.

I will tell you is in contrast with I am not issuing any orders 10 (verse 8). Paul will not employ his apostolic authority in order to obtain money. Their giving must be voluntary, and he now points out why it is in their moral interest to give freely. We must suspect that there was real need to kindle for the first time in Corinth a true spirit of generosity, especially towards a body of Christians in Jerusalem, in whom many would be uninterested. Most tactfully Paul conceals their defect, and yet reveals it, when he indicates that they should go on with this enterprise, for you started it last year. Carry it through suggests a waning enthusiasm. 11 It is in your interest, he says, not to stop what you so readily began. To stop would demoralize them—as every good work does when it begins to drag. It merely uses up energy, tries the temper, and breeds insincerity and formality.

[1] Cf. Seeley, *Ecce Homo*, p. 55.

> Thou hast described
> A hot friend cooling : ever note, Lucilius,
> When love begins to sicken and decay,
> It useth an enforced ceremony.[1]

12, The whole of Paul's argument as to a man not being asked
13 to give what he has not got, nor expected to give so that other
people are to be relieved and you to suffer, is no doubt directed
against certain stock objections and complaints of the ' departing heart,' not so eager as once for the good cause.
The main thing is readiness of heart. Only that is acceptable,
both to God and to the human recipients, which a man gives
14 according to his means, and readily. The words, in order
that their surplus may go to make up what you lack, are
illuminating. Paul speaks to people whose means of livelihood
is uncertain. Their outward condition may alter with political
changes, which they can do nothing to avoid. ' Some day,' he
says, ' you may need from them what they now need from
you.'
15 The relevance of the quotation from Exod. xvi. 18 is not
quite apparent, and is largely verbal. It does not really
illustrate the principle of ' give and take ' as Paul has just
expounded it. It gives little more than a hint that in God's
scheme of things, typified in the manna story, it does not pay
to be selfish ; that serious mistakes may be made by those who
are tenacious of worldly goods, whether they have much or
little. Another suggested translation is, ' The man who took
much gained nothing thereby, and the man who took little
was no loser ' (Gunion Rutherford).

viii. 16–ix. 5 : THE CREDENTIALS OF COLLECTORS, AND THE SPIRIT OF CONTRIBUTORS

16 Thanks be to God who has inspired Titus with an interest in
17 you equal to my own ; he has indeed responded to my
request, but he is off to you by his own choice, so keen is
18 his interest in you. Along with him I am sending that
brother whose services to the gospel are praised by all the

[1] Shakespeare, *Julius Caesar*, IV. ii.

Churches ; besides, he has been appointed by the Churches 19 to travel with me on the business of administering this fund to the glory of the Lord. His appointment has my full consent, for I want to take precautions against any 20 risk of suspicion in connection with the administration of this charity ; I aim at being above reproach not only 21 from God but also from men. Along with them I am also 22 sending our brother : I have had ample proof of his keen interest on many occasions, and it is specially keen on this occasion, as he has absolute confidence in you. Titus is my colleague, he shares my work for you, and these 23 brothers of mine are apostles of the Church, a credit to Christ. So let them have proof of how you can love, and 24 of my reasons for being proud of you ; it will be a proof ix. read by the Churches. Indeed it is quite superfluous for 1 me to be writing to you about this charitable service to the saints ; I know how willing you are, I am proud of it, I 2 have boasted of you to the Macedonians : ' Achaia,' I tell them, ' was all ready last year.' And your zeal has been a stimulus to the majority of them. At the same 3 time I am sending these brothers just in case my pride in you should prove an empty boast in this particular instance ; I want you to be ' all ready,' as I have been telling them that you would be, in case any Macedonians 4 accompany me and find you are not ready—which would make me (not to speak of yourselves) ashamed of having been so sure. That is why I have thought it necessary to 5 ask these brothers to go on in advance and get your promised contribution ready in good time. I want it to be forthcoming as a generous gift, not as money wrung out of you.

These verses represent what may be called the credentials 16- of the three messengers, and give a good example of the con- 24 tents of a ' letter of commendation ' or written certificate (iii. 1). Titus is said to have an interest in you equal to my 16 own, a delicate suggestion that Titus, like Paul, is concerned that the reputation of the Corinthian Church for generosity

17 should stand high. The words, **responded to my request**, might also be rendered ' welcomes our appeal,' i.e. ' to you.' If Dr. Moffatt's rendering be adopted, the meaning would be that Paul, in making the request, found that Titus was prepared
18 to offer his services of his own accord. Various conjectures have been made as to the name of this **brother.** The Fathers suggest Barnabas or Luke. If identification is possible, Luke would be the more likely. He seems to have joined Paul for the first time immediately before he went to Philippi on his first mission there. The first long ' we ' passage in Acts begins at this point (Acts xvi. 10), and Luke may have been left there for some time (Acts xvii. 1). In that case he would be well known to the Macedonian Churches, and an obvious
19 person to select for this mission to Corinth. Whoever the unnamed individual may be, he is evidently a person of some influence and standing. He is the nominee of several Christian communities, and has been formally **appointed** to accompany Paul, in order to convey the money to Jerusalem. The translation of the closing words of the verse in A.V. and R.V. shows that the text wavers between ' my readiness ' and ' your readiness.' The probability is that the former is correct. The meaning is clarified by beginning a new sentence. Paul had readily agreed to have such an influential and trusted person as his companion on such an errand, because he wants
20, 21 **to take precautions** (a strong word) against any charge of maladministration, such as had been alleged by his op-
22 ponents at Corinth (cf. xi. 8, 9, ii. 17). It is impossible even to guess at the name of the third **brother,** who is obviously a
23 personal friend. There is no reason to think that when Paul speaks of the two unnamed envoys, or **apostles of the Churches,**[1] he is making a distinction between them and himself, who is an ' apostle of Christ.' He says of them also that they are **a credit to Christ** ; perhaps rather more strongly, ' a glory to Christ.' There may also be the idea (preserved in the A.V.) that these men are, as it were, mirrors of Christ (cf. iii. 18), ' vessels of His grace and lights of the world ' in their generation. The image and superscription on such lives is

[1] Cf. pp. 41 f.

unmistakably from the royal mint. Paul finds it unnecessary to say so much about Titus. He is already known to them as his fellow-missionary—one **who shares my work for you.** Let 24 these three men have an adequate response to their appeal for money. It will be a practical proof of what Christian love for others means, which they can make known to other Christian Churches. ix.

The repetition which is apparent in chapter ix. has led 1 some commentators to suggest that a fragment of another letter has somehow been inserted here. Other reasons, however, can be assigned for the redundancy. Paul intensifies the urgency of his appeal because he is still uncertain what the Corinthian response will be. This matter of the collection for the saints was evidently put before the Corinthians at an earlier period, but, owing to the trouble that had arisen, had necessarily been set aside (cf. viii. 10). There may have been unwilling givers in Corinth who, out of the difficulties just surmounted, even yet sought to make an excuse for postponing or shelving the whole matter. ' Why make fresh[1,] demands at such a time, when things have just settled down ? '[2] The tone of verses 1–5 suggests that Paul is reminding the Corinthians that at one time they were deeply interested in the scheme, and that he had triumphantly said so in the Macedonian Churches. He does not wish that he should be 3– **made ashamed of having been so sure** and that they themselves 5 should have cause for shame in remembering how zealous they once were. Moreover, just as their zeal at one time had been **a stimulus to the majority** (or ' bulk ') of the Macedonians, so its waning would have a depressing effect on any Macedonians accompanying Paul on his journey to Jerusalem with the money. Apparently the mission, on which Titus and his companions were sent at this time, was in order to reopen the whole question of the contribution, and so to influence their hearts that it might be **a generous gift, not as money wrung out of them.** Neither does Paul want the money to be hurriedly got together when he and his friends arrive on their way to Jerusalem. He hopes that the mission he now sends will set on foot some kind of organized effort.

ix. 6–15 : GIVING IS AN INVESTMENT

6 Mark this : he who sows sparingly will reap sparingly, and he
7 who sows generously will reap a generous harvest. Every-
one is to give what he has made up his mind to give ;
there is to be no grudging or compulsion about it, for God
8 loves the giver who gives cheerfully. God is able to bless
you with ample means, so that you may always have quite
enough for any emergency of your own and ample besides
9 for any kind act to others ; as it is written,

He scatters His gifts to the poor broadcast,
His charity lasts for ever.

10 He who furnishes the sower with seed and with bread to eat
will supply seed for you and multiply it ; He will increase
11 the crop of your charities—you will be enriched on all
hands, so that you can be generous on all occasions, and
your generosity, of which I am the agent, will make men
12 give thanks to God ; for the service rendered by this fund
does more than supply the wants of the saints, it overflows
13 with many a cry of thanks to God. This service shows
what you are, it makes men praise God for the way you
have come under the gospel of Christ which you confess,
and for the generosity of your contributions to themselves
14 and to all ; they are drawn to you and pray for you, on
account of the surpassing grace which God has shown to
15 you. Thanks be to God for His unspeakable gift !

6, These verses carry on the thought of verse 5. ' To give,'
7 says one ancient commentator, ' is not to lose but to sow
seed.' The fruits of true giving are as really guaranteed by
God as the fruits of the earth. To give what he has made
up his mind to give. This excludes merely impulsive giving.
A gift induced by an emotional appeal, either chance or one
deliberately made, is not on the same level as systematic
and thoughtful giving. Emotions die unless they are ' sub-
limated,' allowed to solidify into an eager, intelligent, and
continuous interest in a cause. A gift with grudging or

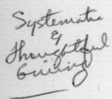

Systematic & Thoughtful Giving

compulsion about it is equally harmful. It means ultimately that we give only when we cannot avoid it. The man who gives cheerfully is the man who has carefully considered the worth of the claim and his own means, and has no subsequent doubts or regrets. Dr. Moffatt's translation, God is able to 8 bless you with ample means, hardly brings out that Paul here again uses the word ' grace ' (*charis*). ' God is able to make every kind of grace to abound in you ' is a more literal translation. The ample means includes not only material things, but the charitable spirit. *Charis* may mean both the gift itself and the spirit or mind of Christ, who is its source. Christianity did not begin as a social movement, but originated in the Person of Jesus Christ. The kind of charity which Paul is urging in these chapters is a new thing in the world, and can have only one source (cf. viii. 9, ix. 15). Paul does not mean to suggest that the man who has most of this world's goods is necessarily the more generous man, if he has the right spirit. The words quite enough for any emergency of your own imply that the generous man, rich or poor, curtails his own wants that he may be able to give to others. The quota- 9 tion from Ps. cxii. 9 is a description of the charitable man. ' Righteousness ' (A.V.) is a technical term for giving (cf. Matt. vi. 1). The farmer's crop does not depend on what he is able 10 to do, but on God. So God will increase the crop of your charities. Part of the crop is men's thanks to God, not 11 merely that the wants of the saints are supplied. The words enriched on all hands, so that you may be generous on all occasions, might rather be rendered ' endowed with a plenitude of generosity,' or, more literally, ' enriched in every respect unto every kind of liberality.' The generous man has ample besides for any kind act to others. Paul's words, are applicable to the liberality which is shown otherwise than in gifts of money. ' A selfish man is never rich. His day is as long as his neighbour's, yet he has no leisure except for his own amusements, no sympathy or concern beyond his own perplexities, no strength but to fight his own battles, and no money except for his own need ; what haunts his mind at every turn is the dread of having too little for himself.'[1] Neither wealth, nor cleverness, nor leisure, nor social position, are necessary endowments for giving on the liberal scale. Gifts that evoke many a cry of thanks to God often characterize lives with little leisure and few endowments.

12- Such God-given enrichment leads men to praise God, and
13 makes the gospel of Christ which you confess more than a creed uttered by the lips. Moreover, this contribution shows what you are. The Jerusalem Church will thereby know the quality of Gentile converts. Such generosity is Christian, from whatever quarter it comes, and, perhaps Paul hints, may have its effect in broadening the theological outlook of some Jewish Christians! The word used in verse 12, translated in R.V. 'ministration' (not 'administration' [A.V.], which would suggest merely arrangements for distribution) and by Dr. Moffatt the service, is a word with an interesting technical meaning. The word is *leitourgia*, and was used of contributions exacted from wealthier citizens in support of the drama (e.g. financing a chorus), in fitting out ships of war, or in training gymnasts. These contributions were a compulsory tax. The word had also come to have a religious meaning, and from it is derived our word 'liturgy.' It is used of the services of the priests and Levites in the Temple and Tabernacle. The word appears in Rom. xv. 27 of this very contribution. 'What Athenian citizens who had the means were made to do, Gentile Christians will be glad to do, in order to render service to society and to God' (Plummer).

14 The idea of service rendered to the community is clearly in Paul's mind. This collection for the saints is more than relief of want. It is for the 'edifying' of the Church. It makes men praise God, changing their mood from despondency to joy. Moreover, it produces religious fellowship between men, turning distant strangers into eager and earnest friends. They are drawn to you, and pray for you, All is God's doing. The fellowship will be the result of the surpassing grace
15 which God has shown to the Gentile Corinthians. Paul has before him this vision of a united, world-wide Christian Church, but it is not merely the wonder of the picture, rather its source,

---

[1] W. M Macgregor, *Jesus Christ the Son of God*, p. 215

which causes him to say, **Thanks be to God for His unspeakable gift!** The unspeakable gift is Jesus Christ. A regal word is used, as in John iv. 10. The **unspeakable** thing, at which we, like Paul himself, can merely throw out words, is that in the Gift, which was all Christ had, God also completely and utterly gave, and gives, Himself. Yet Paul's outburst of praise is no mere indolent ecstasy. It is the climax of a deliberate and elaborate survey of what he has seen men do in the way of sacrificial giving, and of what he knows it is still possible for men to do who have ' first given themselves to the Lord.' He has seen Christ do marvels already with selfish men. Thus is he led by a human road to the threshold of the mystery of Divine giving.[1] The Christ who ' took upon Himself the form of a servant ' is still serving. His Spirit is alive in the hearts of His people.

xiii. 11–14 : The Valediction

Now, brothers, good-bye ; mend your ways, listen to what I 11
    have told you, live in harmony, keep the peace ; then the
    God of love and peace will be with you.
Salute one another with a holy kiss. All the saints salute you. 12–13
The grace of the Lord Jesus Christ and the love of God and the 14
    fellowship of the holy Spirit be with you all.

It is probable that these verses are the close of the letter part of which is contained in chapters i.–ix. Plummer and others regard it as the close of the severe letter. On the whole, the tone of this valediction seems to suit these chapters better.

Salute one another with a holy kiss is really a repetition 12 of the exhortation to peace and harmony in the previous verse, and refers to the meeting for worship. As in the synagogue, the sexes would sit separately. The kiss is ' holy,' as signifying Christian brotherhood.

The Catholic doctrine of the Trinity must not be read back 13 into this verse. There is no reference at all to the mutual relationship of Father, Son, and Holy Spirit. **The grace of the**

[1] Cf. W. M. Macgregor, *op. cit.*, p. 208.

145

Lord Jesus Christ comes first, and the order is significant. It was through the historical revelation of God in Christ that men experienced the Love of God and the new life in the Spirit—a divinely created life of fellowship between God and man, and therefore between man and man, irrespective of race, sex, or social position. This verse is the earliest of the few passages in the New Testament where, in a single sentence, the three elements of the Trinity are set alongside one another. It is significant that, thirty years after Jesus' death, His name, the Holy Spirit, and the name of God Himself should thus be brought together in one benediction. The benediction is a prayer, and the fully developed doctrine of the Trinity has its theological roots in adoration of Jesus Christ.

INDEX OF SUBJECTS

147

INDEX OF AUTHORS